Brad and Angelina

Truth and Lies

CHAS NEWKEY-BURDEN

PENGUIN BOOKS

PENGUIN BOOKS

Published by the Penguin Group
Penguin Books Ltd, 80 Strand, London WC2R ORL, England
Penguin Group (USA) Inc., 375 Hudson Street, New York, New York 10014, USA
Penguin Group (Canada), 90 Eglinton Avenue East, Suite 700, Toronto, Ontario, Canada M4P 2Y3
(a division of Pearson Penguin Canada Inc.)
Penguin Ireland, 25 St Stephen's Green, Dublin 2, Ireland (a division of Penguin Books Ltd)
Penguin Group (Australia), 250 Camberwell Road,
Camberwell, Victoria 3124, Australia (a division of Pearson Australia Group Pty Ltd)
Penguin Books India Pvt Ltd, 11 Community Centre,
Panchsheel Park, New Delhi – 110 017, India
Penguin Group (NZ), 67 Apollo Drive, Rosedale, North Shore 0632, New Zealand
(a division of Pearson New Zealand Ltd)
Penguin Books (South Africa) (Pty) Ltd, 24 Sturdee Avenue,
Rosebank, Johannesburg 2196, South Africa

Penguin Books Ltd, Registered Offices: 80 Strand, London WC2R ORL, England

www.penguin.com

First published in 2010
1

Copyright © Chas Newkey-Burden 2010
See page 247 for a list of picture credits

The moral right of the author has been asserted

Typeset by Penguin Books Ltd
Printed in Great Britain by Clays Ltd, St Ives plc

A CIP catalogue record for this book is available from the British Library

ISBN: 978-0-718-15706-7

www.greenpenguin.co.uk

Mixed Sources
Product group from well-managed
forests and other controlled sources
www.fsc.org Cert no. SA-COC-1592
© 1996 Forest Stewardship Council
FSC

Penguin Books is committed to a sustainable future
for our business, our readers and our planet.
The book in your hands is made from paper
certified by the Forest Stewardship Council.

Brad and Angelina

Contents

Prologue

The arrival of celebrities at the prestigious Directors Guild of America Awards is normally a keenly choreographed affair. Movie superstar Brad Pitt was already inside the Hyatt Regency Plaza for the 2010 ceremony, having masterfully worked the red carpet alongside the renowned director Quentin Tarantino, when the evening's surprise guest swept up dramatically in her chauffeur-driven car. The photographers' flash bulbs went into overdrive and the waiting public craned their necks for a better view as she swung her feet out of the vehicle. When news of the arrival passed into the auditorium the atmosphere became electric. Nobody could quite believe it: Angelina Jolie had arrived. For over a month, intense speculation had mounted that the relationship of the world's most talked-about couple was on the rocks, and when Pitt arrived without her, this did not help to stop the unfounded rumours. The photographers – their faces hidden by their cameras – called Angelina's name, as desperate as ever to capture a money-spinning image of her.

Jolie's unexpected arrival was not only sensational,

it was perplexing. Was this a loving show of support for Pitt, who was to give a speech in honour of Tarantino at the ceremony? And if so, why did they arrive separately, avoiding being photographed together on the red carpet? It was the first time in five years that the couple had refused to pose alongside one another at a showbusiness bash. Just a few months earlier they had spent 45 minutes together on a red carpet, smiling broadly as they were showered by flash lights and questions from the ever-voracious media. But this time Jolie – wearing a green, one-shouldered Elie Saab gown, with Stuart Weitzman shoes and a vintage bag to complete her stunning outfit – walked the carpet without her man, reportedly at the insistence of Pitt.

When Jolie arrived at Pitt's table in the auditorium a hush fell across the room and nearly all eyes were on the couple. Even the self-absorbed great and good of Hollywood were fascinated by the evening's starriest guests. Pitt pulled out a chair for Jolie and she sat next to him, joining the group, which included Tarantino and other movie royalty. 'Brad was doting on her,' said one observer. 'They were very tender together. None of it looked forced.' During the four-hour ceremony, the couple continued to put on a show of happiness and affection, with Pitt touching her back at regular intervals. Every time they touched, other guests stared and whispered to each other, prompting Jolie to fiddle nervously with her Ofira Schwartz gold earrings. It was claimed that it was only when Pitt began drinking that the glow between them momentarily darkened.

'They were extremely affectionate,' said another onlooker. After the ceremony all talk was about the 'super-couple' and their show of unity in the face of growing conjecture about their relationship. It is so much more than a relationship though. As the most discussed couple of the twenty-first century, they have become a fearsome, all-conquering brand, dubbed 'Brangelina'. From the very start of their love affair a media storm has surrounded them, one that quickly became so extreme that the prestigious press agency Reuters declared it had 'reached the point of insanity'. Indeed, when they were expecting their first child together the media described it as the most eagerly anticipated birth since Jesus Christ.

Their tactile, affectionate behaviour throughout the Directors Guild ceremony might have stopped tongues wagging over their alleged difficulties, but only temporarily. At the end of the evening they once again refused to be photographed together and, getting into different cars, left the ceremony separately. It had been a glamorous, showbusiness evening full of surprises, fascinated speculation and conflicting signals as all eyes focused on two people.

Business as usual, then, for the man and woman whose relationship would make for a superb, block-busting movie and who together make up the thrilling phenomenon that is Brangelina . . .

1. Brad: Hollywood's Golden Boy

When he first pulled up in Los Angeles to try and break into the movie industry, Brad Pitt's prospects seemed as bleak as those of many Hollywood hopefuls. The twenty-two-year-old university dropout had little acting experience and almost no contacts in the world of cinema. Few observers would have rated his chances of becoming one of the globe's most successful and instantly recognizable actors. It would have seemed more likely that he would end up as another Los Angeles cliché, waiting restaurant tables as his dream of a big break slowly set over the Hollywood hills. However, Pitt was a boyishly handsome young man with considerable reserves of ambition, focus and energy, and as a Sagittarian he is also said by astrologists to have a naturally optimistic attitude. If so, it would serve him well in the years ahead. Perhaps it was his wholesome, Midwestern ways that helped charm the denizens of Tinseltown, followed by the world at large.

William Bradley Pitt was born on 18 December 1963 in Shawnee, a city in the Pottawatomie County of Oklahoma, right in the heart of the American

Midwest. It couldn't have been a more different world to the coastal showbusiness metropolises of Los Angeles and New York that would eventually become his natural habitat.

In contrast to the many Hollywood stars who have followed in the footsteps of thespian parents, Pitt was treading entirely unfamiliar territory with his chosen career path. His father, William Alvin, was an executive of a small trucking company and his mother, Jane, worked in education. William Bradley was their first child and friends of the family quickly recognized in him the looks of his father and the character of his mother. Although they named their son after his father, he soon became known simply by a derivative of his middle name, Brad. The family moved soon after his birth to Springfield in Missouri after William received a more tempting job offer from a different firm, and Pitt has accurately described the town as 'a very white-bread Christian community'.

Pitt was followed at neat three-year intervals by two siblings: brother Doug arrived in 1966 and the boys were joined by a sister, Julie Neal, in 1969. The family was a tight unit and theirs was a happy home, a far cry from the tortured childhoods that are claimed by a growing number of actors in publicity-gathering tell-all interviews and memoirs. The Pitt siblings were friendly and fond of one another, and Julie remembers thinking that her brothers were 'the greatest things that ever happened'.

Theirs was a conservative, religious home, but not in an extreme or fundamentalist fashion. His parents are members of the Southern Baptist Convention, which became the world's largest Baptist denomination after splitting with the northern Baptists in 1845. The religious tone they set influenced Pitt from an early age. 'I always had a lot of questions about the world, even in kindergarten,' he has said. 'A big question to me was fairness. If I'd grown up in some other religion, would I get the same shot at Heaven as a Christian has?' He might have pondered these questions as the family attended the South Haven Baptist Church every Sunday, but he was often so bored during services that he used to fantasize about noisily breaking wind and proudly claiming the credit for it. Thankfully, he got himself noticed in a happier way. It was at the age of just six that the future big-screen star began to stand out from the crowd in church, according to church pianist Connie Bilyeu. 'You couldn't keep from watching Brad because his face was so expressive,' she remembers.

Pitt's third grade teacher, Jan Woodland, also recalls with a smile 'sweet little Brad' and his 'big old blue eyes and dimples'. According to Woodland, far from being a show-off, the future movie star was a rather reserved boy at his independent day school, Horace

Mann Elementary. 'He didn't have to show off or be a smart alec to stand out,' she said. 'He was shy and laid back, the kind of kid you wanted your little girls to like.'

Little could Woodland have guessed what colourful experiences young Pitt was having away from school. One day he and some friends found a pile of top-shelf *Playboy* magazines at a building site where they were playing. It was an abrupt sexual awakening for the youngsters. 'Well, I was very impressed,' remembered Pitt of the experience. He was less impressed when his mother drew him some clinical diagrams one day to explain what 'sexual intercourse' was after they had both overheard some children using the 'f' word. 'I remember vividly, at that time, being horrified,' he said of this latest visual instalment of his sexual education. It must have been an awkward conversation for his mother too.

By the time he moved on to high school, Pitt was already proving popular with the opposite sex and he held 'make-out' parties in the basement of the family home to which heavily lip-glossed girls eagerly flocked. He attended the memorably titled Kickapoo High School, which is named after a Native American tribe and has the attention-grabbing unofficial slogan 'Fear the Poo!' With his boyish good looks, young Brad was never short of attention from the fairer sex and was voted the 'Best Dressed Student' in the school yearbook. The first signs of his heart-melting romantic side came after he developed a crush on a classmate called Sara Hart. One winter's day, following a heavy snow shower, he drew a large heart in the snow outside Sara's classroom, writing 'Hi Sara' in the middle of the heart. No wonder he was so popular with the girls.

'He always had lots of dates,' former classmate Mark Swadley recalled. Pitt had a particular eye for blondes. Not only did he enjoy lots of dates, he also ended up scrapping with male classmates over the most popular girls in the school. As he later readily admitted, he wasn't the most fearsome of combatants. 'I had the usual sorts of fights over girls. From memory, I won one – probably because I took a cheap shot like grabbing the guy's nuts, or something – and lost one. The only serious damage was to my ego.' Happier times came when he was selected to pose for the school's calendar, the first photo shoot in a life that was soon to be dominated by the flashing bulb of the camera. He was also voted in as the student body's public relations officer and displayed noticeable leadership skills from an early age. 'He was a good leader, well liked in the school cabinet, where he promoted all the dances and spirit days,' recalled Swadley.

This portrait of a budding heart-throb and all-round good egg is enriched by the fact that Pitt was an athletic youngster. He loved playing sport and was particularly adept on the golf course, the tennis court and in the swimming pool. Not that he was only a hit as an athlete, he was also a persuasive force in the school's debating society, where his ability to perform and captivate an audience first became evident. Pitt also sang in the school choir and got a few minor parts in some school plays, though there was no hint of the future film star in his performances. As the Pitt family's former pastor Reverend Paul Swadley – father of Pitt's classmate Mark – succinctly put it to *People* magazine: '[Brad] didn't steal the spotlight.'

He did, however, develop a growing love of cinema. The first film he can remember seeing is *Butch Cassidy and the Sundance Kid*, and he also recalls being captivated by *Ordinary People*, *Saturday Night Fever* and *Planet of the Apes*. Pitt watched the latter movie during a re-run at a drive-in cinema as a family treat. He sat with a cup of soft drink and a tub of popcorn resting on his lap, on the face of it no different to the other children present. However, the lure of the big screen was beginning to clutch the youngster.

Not that he believed a career in cinema was on the cards for him. At this stage in his life Pitt's most burning ambition was to work on the creative side of the advertising industry. True, he also dreamt of becoming a rock star, but so do many men in their late teenage years. He loved The Who and Elton John as a youngster and his fondness for rock music of an increasingly cutting-edge variety continues to this day.

After graduating from high school he enrolled at the University of Missouri in Columbia, where he began studying for a journalism degree. He was 150 miles from home, but in a good place for such studies – the University was the first in the world to open a designated school of journalism in 1908 and they were good and proud times for the school. Among his fellow students there was a young man called James Grimaldi, who has since become a Pulitzer Prize-winning investigative reporter for the *Washington Post*.

It was an eye on commercialism as much as creativity that made Pitt focus on the advertising modules of the course, and away from his studies, he continued some of the pursuits he had enjoyed at high school. In his spare time, he would sometimes act in fraternity shows, again without bringing the house down. His handsome looks continued to turn heads, though, and he was asked to pose for a calendar, appearing shirtless as 'Mr December' in the 1983–4 'Men of Mizzou' calendar. He also took part in a charity strip show, which hundreds of girls paid to watch. 'He was the hottest guy in the country,' said a fellow stripper, recalling the excitement. Another fellow student revealed that Pitt was part of a seven-man troupe called the Dancing Bares when he was a member of fraternity Sigma Chi. Thomas Whelihan told *In Touch Weekly*, 'When a girl from one of our sister sororities turned twenty-one, the Bares would put her in a chair and come out butt-naked with pillowcases on their heads and do a choreographed dance for her. The girls would be laughing so hard. It was great!'

This was quite a new way of life for Pitt after his Baptist-based small-town upbringing. Away from his pious household Pitt's attitude to life was changing. A fellow Missouri student remembers Pitt as a slightly rough-looking young man, hanging around a local pizza restaurant asking where the evening's parties were going to be held. He was not living the fully debauched lifestyle of the rock star he dreamt of becoming, but he was dipping his toe into that world. Accordingly, Pitt revealed that around this time he began to question some of the religious beliefs he had been raised with. 'When I got untethered from the comfort of religion, it wasn't a loss of faith for me, it was a discovery of self,' he said. 'I had faith that I'm capable enough to handle any situation. There's peace in understanding that I have only one life, here and now, and I'm responsible.' He was about to seize control of his life, taking a dramatic new direction. It constituted a definite risk, but his eyebrow-raising audacity would be fruitfully rewarded as he supported the belief that fortune favours the brave.

To the surprise of his family and friends, Pitt dropped out of university when he was just two credits short of completing his degree. It was less than a fortnight till graduation, yet he threw years of work away in order to chase his real dream: acting on the big screen. It was quite a turnaround. A car crash he had recently been involved in had served as a wake-up call for the young man, reminding him how short and fragile life can be. 'I had this sinking feeling as graduation approached,' he recalled. 'I saw my friends getting jobs. I wasn't ready to settle down. I loved films. They were a portal into different worlds for me, and Missouri wasn't where movies were made. Then it hit me: if they didn't come to me, I'd go to them.' He waved goodbye to his fellow students and packed his belongings into his trusty silver Nissan, nick-named Runaround Sue after Dion's 1960s number one. With just $325 to his name the twenty-two-year-old hit the road with Led Zeppelin, Jimi Hendrix and Lynryd Skynyrd playing the soundtrack on his long road trip to Hollywood.

Like most of the people who have dropped it all to chase success in Tinseltown, Pitt started his new life there by taking distinctly unglamorous jobs. One of the earliest was as a chauffeur for strippers. 'My job was to drive them to bachelor parties and things,' he remembered. 'I'd pick them up, and at the gig I'd collect the money, play the bad Prince tapes and catch the girls' clothes. It wasn't a wholesome atmosphere and it got very depressing.' He also took a job dressing up as a giant chicken to promote the El Pollo Loco restaurant on Sunset Boulevard, dancing around in the outfit in front of the restaurant. It was degrading work, but he considered the $9 an hour pay respectable compared to the $3.50 hourly rate he'd received for previous jobs. When bawdy diners hurled insults and abuse at him, he took a deep breath and shrugged it off. They weren't shouting at him, he told himself, they were shouting at the chicken.

Pitt still harboured ambitions to be a rock star and had fallen in with a circle of musicians with whom he'd jam on guitar. Movies, though, remained his number one dream, and he was about to get a big hand-up into that industry from one of the strippers he'd been driving round town. She referred him to the studio of acting coach Roy London, who had guided stars like Sharon Stone to success. Pitt was delighted – it was exactly the sort of break he'd been hoping for.

On arrival at London's studio, Pitt – who had let himself go a touch in recent times – didn't come across as the heart-throb he would become. But he had charisma, recalled one of the instructors, Ivana Chubbuck. 'He had more pounds on him then, and he wasn't as good-looking,' she said. Others from the same time recall differently, though. At six-foot tall and with a wonderfully square jaw he was quite an eyeful, even when not at his most handsome. Besides, he had a charm that could melt hearts. Indeed, the mother of one of his friends described him as 'a Roman God' the first time she encountered him. Even Chubbuck admits, 'There was definitely something about him that was special.' That special something first showed itself in a scene he was asked to perform early on in his days at the studio, although it seemed to be more natural than contrived. Pitt, who was learning the ropes fast, was handed the brief to play the part of a shy man, sharing a picnic with a woman he was attracted to. 'He was standing up offering her some wine and twisting the stems in a very sexual manner,' said Chubbuck. 'It was all subconscious. He was very unaware of what he had done, and when I told him, he just blushed.'

This prim performance was mirrored in the real world, too, where Pitt was more focused on work than women. His ambition was steely and tangible to those around him. He remained something of a loner at the studio, behaving with an aloof focus that contrasted starkly with the partying ways of many of his fellow wannabe actors. As Chubbuck put it, Pitt was 'a hard, hard worker'. The dating days of high school and the party life of university seemed an age ago as he eschewed the hard-playing ways of his classmates, preferring to stay behind and rehearse a scene for the following day. Sometimes Chubbuck would ask him whether any young ladies had caught his eye. 'And he'd say, "No, there's no one,"' she remembers. 'He was so unaware of that part of who he was.'

Pitt worked hard and had natural ability, but in the painfully competitive world of Hollywood nothing comes easy. First he had to endure some demoralizing roles as a 'supporting artist', otherwise known as an 'extra', in the 1987 films *Less Than Zero* – in which we wore a pink and white striped tank top and earned just $38 – *No Man's Land* and *No Way Out*. They were uncredited, minor roles that gave him only the merest taste of what he really wanted, and he later described some of them as 'butt-awful'.

On the small screen he appeared in the sitcom *Growing Pains* and this guest part landed him a four-episode run in CBS's hit soap opera *Dallas*. He admitted he got 'sweaty palms' ahead of filming his scenes as 'an idiot boyfriend who gets caught in the hay'. The special something that had been noted in him at the acting studio was also noticed by producer Patrick Hasburgh, who cast him for a minor television role in 1988 after a memorable audition. 'Brad walking into a room was more exciting than most actors doing a scene,' he said.

Women continued to be excited by Pitt, too. His manager in the late 1980s was a man called Phil Lobel, and he remembers Pitt dating many beautiful women during this time, sometimes borrowing money in order to buy the expensive presents he enjoyed showering on his latest flame. 'He fell in love very easily,' said Lobel of his romantic client. Friends noticed that Pitt's somewhat shy nature didn't seem to be a barrier to meeting new women, because they were only too happy to approach him in the first instance.

One woman he was briefly involved with around this time was British pop star Sinitta, who shot to fame with her single 'So Macho' in 1986. 'We only had a brief affair,' said Sinitta, who also used to date reality television superstar Simon Cowell and who works as one of his sidekicks on *The X Factor* now, 'but it was wonderfully passionate.'

Pitt dated actress Robin Givens for six months in 1989 and nearly ended up in hot water when, as he arrived at her home one evening brandishing wine and gifts, he ran into her ex-husband, champion heavyweight boxer Mike Tyson. Fortunately Givens managed to diffuse the tension and no punches were thrown in what would have been a very uneven duel. Another Hollywood actress he dated for a while was Jill Schoelen, who he met on the set of horror film *Cutting Class*. A more serious relationship developed between him and Juliette Lewis, his co-star in *Too*

Young to Die?, who was then sixteen to Pitt's twenty-six. They immediately fell for each other and were soon sharing a small rented bungalow in Los Angeles. Lewis in particular was reportedly very 'intense' about their relationship, describing her man as 'like a painting'.

The couple were soon considering marriage, with Pitt denying at the time that their shared profession was ever likely to become a barrier to their happiness. 'Our lives are not our work,' he insisted. 'We were trying to be Sid and Nancy or something,' he said, looking back at the early stages of their relationship when they went for a rebellious grunge look at Los Angeles bashes. Ironically, the parts they played in *Too Young to Die?* were of a romantic drug-fuelled coupling. 'Yeah, it was quite romantic,' Pitt joked of his part, 'shooting her full of drugs and stuff.'

In the meantime, however, Pitt was about to land the role that would change his life. He wasn't first choice for the part of J. D. in the road movie *Thelma and Louise*, but when William Baldwin dropped the part to appear in another movie, director Ridley Scott called Pitt to audition for the relatively minor role. 'It just sparked,' said Pitt of his reading, and he was given the part. He enjoyed the slightly anarchic atmosphere on set, saying that Scott would 'play around' with the cast a lot. But despite being involved in a very passionate love-making scene in the film, he found the experience entirely unromantic to shoot. For a start he was worried about what his mother would think when she learned of the scene, and he also recalled the crew noticing a zit on his buttocks one day, leading him to be pounced upon by a make-up lady with a toothbrush and concealer. 'It just makes me laugh,' he said. 'It's the classic thing – you know, before a school picture you get a zit . . . I mean, how seriously can you take it all?' Pitt recalls a similar experience when filming a scene in another film when his character relieves himself into a bucket. He was asked to let it flow again for the benefit of the sound crew, who all crowded round to capture the acoustics.

Thelma and Louise was a huge hit and female cinema-goers were enraptured by his love scene, which was also a stand-out moment for many of the critics, with *Rolling Stone* purring admiringly over his portrayal of 'a hitchhiking hunk'. Among those who watched the film was a young lady called Jennifer Aniston, and a sixteen-year-old Angelina Jolie, whose eyes widened with approval during Pitt's romping scene.

In the wake of the film Pitt drew comparisons with James Dean, who he had first been compared with in 1989 after his appearance in *Tales from the Crypt*. It seemed his sex symbol status had been cemented and he has since described the scene as 'the $6,000 orgasm'. In truth it was to be worth much more to him than that, both on and off screen. He was becoming the man who could do no wrong in the eyes of many women. Even when he piled on 20 pounds and grew a greasy beard in order to play a serial killer in the movie *Kalifornia*, he still entranced the women on set. 'This guy just gets through to women, no matter what,' noticed *Kalifornia* director Dominic Sena. He even had admirers in the lesbian community, including gay singer Melissa Etheridge, who said she and some fellow lesbians had agreed that Pitt was one man who could 'turn' them straight for an evening.

Working on *Thelma and Louise* had been an educational experience for Pitt. The cast included the likes of Harvey Keitel and Susan Sarandon. 'They were fun and exciting,' he purred. 'It's like when you play tennis with someone better than you – your game gets better.'

It helped prepare him for a film that the *Los Angeles Times* would describe as a 'career-making performance'. First, though, he had to endure the discomfort of successive disappointments, when his next two films, *Johnny Suede* and *Cool World*, flopped commercially and critically. He was then cast by Robert Redford – an actor he had often been compared with – to star in his biographical film *A River Runs Through It*. It was the first time Pitt had been asked to front a classy, mainstream film. 'I felt a bit of pressure on *A River*

Runs Through It,' said the actor. 'And I thought that it was one of my weakest performances. It's so weird that it ended up being the one that I got the most attention for.'

Away from work, Pitt was ready to call time on his relationship with Lewis. He had been concerned for a while that the intensity of her feelings for him continued to exceed his, and when she got involved with the controversial Church of Scientology, it was the last straw for Pitt. 'Oh boy,' he sighed when *Empire* magazine later asked him about Scientology. 'Don't get me started! I'd go on for a couple of hours about that. The thirty-second version is: I'm not big on anything that tells you how to live your life.'

Pitt packed his belongings into his car, including his guitar collection, some antiques and a beloved espresso machine, and drove off to a new life. At first he lived alone in a rented flat, living the bachelor lifestyle in much the same way as he'd lived during his university years, but even more laid back. At night he would either slouch in front of television films or trawl the bars of Los Angeles, picking up girls who would willingly follow him back home.

He was in no hurry to find a new permanent home for himself, but eventually chose a 1910 Craftsman property in the famous Hollywood hills. After the cramped home he had shared with Lewis, and the temporary flat he moved to afterwards, this was his first chance to make his mark on a property and turn a house into a home. It was a fine property with a rooftop terrace, balconies and a pool. There was even a man-made cave in the garden, in which he kept forty chameleons in cages. He also acquired three dogs, to whom he gave the curious names Saudi, Purty and Todd Potter. The mutts would soon be joined by a pair of bobcats, courtesy of the arrival of Pitt's latest flame, Jitka Pohlodek, a twenty-four-year-old Czech actress he met at a party. 'Yit', as he affectionately nicknamed her, soon moved in with him, bringing her bobcats with her. The couple spent little time together as Pitt was working on two new films, *Legends of the Fall* and *Interview With a Vampire*. Once more, conflicting schedules proved to make romantic life difficult for Pitt.

The latter film proved to be something of an albatross for Pitt. 'I hated doing this movie,' he later admitted. Controversy over the casting of his opposite number Tom Cruise cast the first shadow over proceedings. Then River Phoenix, who had a small role in the film, died of a drug overdose before filming his part. As for Pitt, he claimed never to have been a particular fan of substance abuse. 'The drug thing is out,' he said. 'I've experimented with all kinds of lifestyles, but you either quit drugs or you die.'

Tragedy struck the set again when the mother of one of the crew died during the making of the film, causing Pitt to question whether the big screen could ever truly portray real-life bereavement. 'It's pretty much bullshit, really, what we do,' he concluded. He also disliked spending nearly six months playing the part of a depressed character. 'I gotta find a comedy next, man, or I'll break out the razor blades,' he said. No doubt his mood wasn't helped by the damning verdicts he received from the critics when the film was released. 'Pitt remains a whining, monotonous killjoy,' declared the *Daily Mail* unkindly. Despite everything, though, the film was a commercial success, taking Pitt ever higher on the ladder of success.

Following his split from Jitka Pohlodek, Pitt moved on to a relationship which proved to be more successful and certainly more high profile. He was cast in the crime film *Se7en* as the husband of a character played by Gwyneth Paltrow. The on-screen couple soon became lovers in real life, causing a dream to come true for Paltrow, who had held a torch for Pitt since watching *Thelma and Louise* as a fifteen-year-old and thinking, Who is that gorgeous guy? When they started filming together in December 1994, the potent chemistry between them was palpable. '[It] was real,' said co-star Morgan Freeman. The spark was first struck when they dined at an Italian restaurant in Los Angeles one night. 'The romance grew from there,' revealed Paltrow. 'I was charmed by his intelligence and sensitivity, his closeness to his family and the way in which he was completely down to earth.' There was growing cause for him *not* to be that way, and not just because of his acting achievements. He was named 'Sexiest Man Alive' by *People* magazine in 1995 and then British gay magazine *Attitude* ranked him top of their 'Twenty Sexiest Men' readers' poll. Such incredible success came with a price, though.

The same year, Pitt and Paltrow were handed a stark reminder of how fascinated the media was by their relationship. They holidayed on the exclusive Caribbean island of St Barts. One lazy, hot afternoon, believing they were in an entirely private area, the couple lounged naked by the pool. To their horror they later discovered they'd been photographed by a French paparazzo and that the images were soon to be published in a French magazine, then a British tabloid newspaper before also being spread across the worldwide web. 'It was horrendous,' said Pitt. He felt angry and hurt for himself, but was particularly protective of Paltrow, saying, 'I see how it hurts her.' She was indeed hurt, and furious too, saying of the gentlemen of the British tabloid press, 'They are the most hideous creatures on the face of the Earth.' In January of 1996, the couple were again rocked when the *National Enquirer* was leaked details of Pitt's marriage proposal to Paltrow, and the fact that she had declined.

At thirty-two years of age, the previously fearful-of-commitment Pitt had eschewed settling down, but now felt ready. In December, he drove Paltrow to a quiet park, deep in the Hollywood hills, where he wined and dined her in a romantic restaurant in a beautiful mansion within the park. He then fixed her with a serious stare and asked her to marry him on New Year's Eve. The couple were due to spend Christmas with his family back in Missouri, and he hoped to break the exciting news of their engagement on arrival. He was disappointed when, after a moment's shocked silence, she said no. Paltrow, who was twenty-three years old at this stage, explained she wasn't ready for such a level of commitment. She pointed to the experiences of other Hollywood couples who had married young. 'It usually doesn't last more than two years,' she said. Although Paltrow wasn't ready to get engaged to the world's sexiest man, they remained together as a couple and were spotted, despite Pitt's efforts to hide under a yellow turban, house-hunting in the wealthy area of the Hamptons. In January 1996, he thanked Paltrow during his acceptance speech for a Golden Globe award for Best Supporting Actor, for his part in the science fiction film *Twelve Monkeys*, describing her as 'my angel, the love of my life'. This was his first major award, though he had been nominated for a Best Actor Golden Globe for his part in *Legends of the Fall*.

He continued to try to convince Paltrow to marry him, proposing a total of four times before she finally agreed. She was visiting him in Argentina, where he was filming *Seven Years in Tibet*, when he presented her with a $35,000 diamond ring that he'd designed and commissioned especially for her. This time she said yes, and in response he quickly snapped up the neighbouring properties to his home, hoping to create a fortress for them to live in. Between them the properties cost $1million, the same price he reportedly splashed out on a mansion for them near the King's Road in Chelsea, west London. 'This last year I've been as happy as I've ever been,' he announced. So when the engagement was called off and the relationship terminated, it shocked the show-business world.

Rival theories emerged for the breakdown of their relationship: she felt pressured by him or vice versa; the entire engagement had been a hoaxed publicity stunt; the pressure of living in the public eye had destroyed their love; long spells spent apart had caused a rift. To add to his discomfort, soon after their split, the naked photographs from their Caribbean holiday resurfaced in the media. All the while his ex-girlfriend Lewis continued to publicly talk about their broken relationship even though it had ended three years earlier. As recently as 2007 she was still speaking out about him, reportedly telling a fellow drinker in a bar that Pitt 'was no . . . big deal, if ya know what I mean!'

Pitt had never been comfortable with life in the public eye, and even got frustrated by innocuous interviews with teen magazines. 'It's like: "What's your favourite colour?" I don't know! I like a bunch of 'em,' he complained. Not that he was fond of more serious questions either. During an interview with a more grown-up publication while promoting *Seven Years in Tibet*, Pitt was scornful of the idea that actors should pronounce on political issues. 'Reporters ask me what I feel China should do about Tibet,' he said. 'Who cares what I feel China should do about Tibet? I'm a fucking actor! They hand me a script. I act. Basically, when you whittle everything away, I'm a grown man who puts on make-up.' How dramatically his position on this would change when he came under the influence of Angelina Jolie.

Pitt has rarely been comfortable being recognized in public, least of all when he was preparing to film the Ulster thriller *The Devil's Own* and was beaten up by two Irish Republicans who spotted him glancing in the window of a Protestant-run bookshop. With the media following his every move, life could never be the same for the man from Missouri. While growing up he hadn't experienced or learned how to deal with fame and intrusion. All his family still lived in Missouri and led normal, quiet lives, while his every move was dissected by the world's media. His break-up with Paltrow was a lead item on America's top news networks long before celebrity stories were routinely covered in this way.

All this media controversy didn't alter Pitt's standing as Hollywood's new golden boy, whose easy charm had won over the industry and the paying public. The offers continued to flood in and he was, at this stage, typically earning over $12 million a film. How far he'd come since receiving just $38 for tiny parts as an extra. He was creatively stretching himself as an actor, too. For his part as an Austrian mountaineer in *Seven Years in Tibet* Pitt learned and practised real-life rock climbing in California and the Alps. There was more 'method acting' on show for his role in *Fight Club*, where he learned boxing and a variety of martial arts. He also had part of his front teeth chipped out prior to filming to lend him a more authentic street-fighter look, only restoring his teeth to their former glory after the wrap.

This story captured the press's attention, giving a new angle to the heart-throb of Hollywood, but the story that really fascinated the media was his latest romantic relationship, which started in the summer of 1998. At first his new dalliance seemed like a rebound fling after his split from Paltrow. Once more Pitt was dating a famous actress, but this time they seemed made for each other, and it appeared when they married that he'd finally found true, lasting happiness with a young woman who, despite her fame and good looks, remained the girl next door at heart . . .

2. The Girl Next Door

While Pitt was smooching his way through elementary school in Missouri, over on the West Coast of America a girl was born who was destined to become a star and play a high-profile romantic role in his life. Unlike Pitt, Jennifer Aniston was born into show-business, not only geographically, hailing from the Los Angeles suburb of Sherman Oaks, but in terms of her family heritage. Her father, Yannis Anastassakis, came from Crete but changed his name to John Aniston when he moved to America with his parents as a young boy. His father reportedly decided on the new surname for the family as they drove through Anniston, Alabama. Keen to make it big as an actor in the land of opportunity, he appeared in Broadway plays while still a teenager and then during his twenties started to appear on TV as well, including Second World War drama *Combat!* He married an actress, Nancy Dow, who was divorced with a three-year-old son. She and John had their first child together, Jennifer, on 11 February 1969, and she was to have a famous godfather: the iconic star of television crime drama *Kojak*, Telly Savalas, who like John had Greek roots and was a close family friend. On the day of Aniston's baptism at an orthodox Greek ceremony, Savalas lovingly held her, whispering reassuring words into her ear. Following the ceremony he held her in the back seat of his Rolls-Royce. Aniston, who had taken a tot of wine during the baptism, vomited over her godfather's black velvet dinner jacket and then again all over the plush seats of the car. He remained a loving godfather, though, giving her lollipops as treats and even buying her a bike one year as a present.

However, this was no golden showbusiness tale as both of Jennifer's parents struggled to find exciting acting roles. A particularly cruel blow was dealt John after he was lined up to take a major part in the *Mary Tyler Moore* television show, only to be replaced at the last minute by actor Ted Knight. Poor John was forced to watch while Knight collected a string of Emmy awards during the show's run, which lasted seven years. In the wake of this bitter disappointment, John was dropped by his agent. Savalas rushed to his friend's aid, handing him guest appearances in *Kojak*, but the family continued to struggle financially. Aniston was largely unaware of these problems, enjoying the simple pleasure of playing with her Barbie dolls. Under pressure from his wife, John eventually dropped acting to enter the medical profession. The Anistons moved back to Greece for John to study at the university, and lived in Athens until a local conflict forced them to return to America. Turkey had invaded Cyprus and occupied part of the island, forcing the closure of the island's university. This led to an influx of Cypriot students arriving at the University of Athens, where John had yet to complete his studies. Since priority was given to the displaced Cypriot students, John found himself out on his ear for the time being at least.

The family returned to America, where John initially intended to continue his medical studies. However, they soon moved to New York where he'd managed to secure a role in the successful television soap opera *Love of Life*. For Nancy New York was familiar terrain as she'd grown up in the Big Apple, but living on the Upper West Side of Manhattan was a new experience for Jennifer. She was a resident of perhaps the most exciting city in the world, with a view from her window of the famous Empire State Building and a famous father with even more famous friends. Life should have been a joy for a girl like her, but she wasn't entirely fond of her new home, describing the neighbourhood as 'pretty seedy', which in those days it was. Nor could the showbusiness glitter mask the domestic pain that was in store for Jennifer as she grew up. She'd observed a lot of Greek men treating their wives badly during the family's stay in Athens. 'Women are still second-class citizens [there],' she has claimed. 'Greek men are well known for being philanderers.' The family might have left Greece, but as she would soon discover, to her horror, those chauvinistic views had followed them back to America.

Still, when times were good for the family, they were very good. She recalls periods when the house would resonate with laughter and happiness, and both her parents had contagious laughs. 'When one would start, the other would follow,' she remembered. 'There's nothing better than contagious laughter. It's the most peaceful feeling in the world.' She felt, she said, 'fearless' as a seven-year-old. The perfect family picture was completed by visits to the exclusive Hamptons beach resort, where Jennifer befriended a boy called Michael. One day Michael's grandfather encouraged the lad to give Aniston a kiss, though he proved too shy to act on the suggestion. Aniston was a warm child and strolled over to Michael, planting a friendly kiss on him instead. Strange to think that she would return to the Hamptons later in life, house-hunting with one of the most famous men on the planet. This seeming blissful existence was about to become shattered when her parents split, though. For the first but not final time in her life, Aniston was going to learn the hard way that just when things seem perfect, they can unravel and become very messy.

*

In 1978, her father John fell for his *Love of Life* co-star Sherry Rooney. In many ways Rooney was similar to Nancy. A slender brunette, she too had a moderately successful acting career, having taken a small role in one film and also appeared in a television soap opera called *Search for Tomorrow*. Nancy and perhaps Jennifer had noticed that John seemed to be spending more and more time away from home, but both were shocked to the core when they learned he was leaving the family for Rooney. The day Aniston was told, she had been having fun at the birthday party of a friend when her mother, wearing sunglasses to conceal her tear-stained eyes, arrived to collect her. When they got home, her mother told Jennifer that her father would not be at home for a while. 'I just remember sitting there crying, not understanding that he was gone,' Jennifer later told *Rolling Stone* magazine. Nancy recalled that as she broke the news, 'I watched a tear roll down Jenny's cheek as confidence faded from her once trusting eyes.'

Jennifer recalls that only some months later was she told the full truth about the break-up and where her father now lived. At the time she blamed herself for the split, which might seem harsh but is a common response from children of divorced parents. The divorce was completed in August 1980, and in 1984 John married Rooney. Aniston would visit her father at their new home in New Jersey, but the visits weren't always happy. One day, as father and daughter ate together at the dining room table, he sent Jennifer to her room for not being sufficiently entertaining conversationally. 'My father told me I had nothing to say,' she recalled. 'He made me leave the table.' It was an upsetting moment for the young Aniston and only served to encourage her to become more interesting and to pursue the creative development she had already been working on. That said, she did rebel at school at times, but only because she hoped that if she was naughty enough, then both her parents would be called to the principal's office – something she hoped might spark a reunion. No such thing was forthcoming, though, and instead Jennifer was raised single-handedly by her mother who, under the strain, would often lose her temper and scream at her daughter.

At the age of nine, one of Aniston's paintings was chosen to be hung in the prestigious New York Metropolitan Museum of Art. Her creative urges were simmering inside her and when she was taken to see *Children of a Lesser God* on Broadway one Sunday afternoon, she decided to channel those urges into becoming an actress. 'I was sitting in the second or third row,' she told *Rolling Stone* magazine, 'and I was blown away. I walked out saying, "That's what I want to do."' She enrolled in her school's drama club – she attended the fee-paying Rudolf Steiner school, an establishment known for encouraging creativity in its pupils – and took part in a nativity play, playing an angel. The school she attended discouraged its pupils from watching television at home, but when her half brother John Melick babysat her she would sneakily get to watch *The Bionic Woman*. She liked what she saw. 'She'd make that ba-na-na-na-na sound effect around the house, running around directing herself in scenes from the show,' said Melick. Then in 1984, at the age of fifteen, she applied, along with 3,000 other youngsters, for the seventy places up for grabs at New York's High School for Performing Arts, the very place that inspired the popular musical television series and film *Fame*. She was showing her father that she was indeed an interesting person, but he wasn't pleased by her showbusiness ambitions. 'I don't think a father who knows anything about this business would be thrilled to have a daughter who is in it,' he has said.

Jennifer also wisely prepared a back-up plan by studying psychology in the evenings, just in case her acting ambitions didn't come true. She also took various part-time jobs, including waitressing in a Manhattan burger restaurant and working as a bike courier. It was hard combining all these different and demanding pursuits, and she was pleased to rest her head on the pillow each evening in the apartment she was renting in Manhattan's West Village.

Happily, her dedication began to pay off in time, and she started to get parts in various plays. First an off-off-Broadway production called *Dancing On Checkers' Grave* when she was nineteen years of age, then moving to off-Broadway in *For Dear Life*, written by the award-winning playwright Susan Miller. When the Billboard sheets were printed for these plays, the cast was listed alphabetically, so even though she wasn't the most experienced member of the cast, she was nearly always listed at the top. They were all short-running plays, though, and Jennifer found Broadway as difficult as ever to crack, causing her to eventually follow the well-trodden path to Hollywood, where she would try her luck in the movie world.

Aniston's move wasn't as flushed with risk as the one taken by Pitt, since her father and stepmother lived in Tinseltown by this time, so she could stay with them in relative security. All the same, like Pitt she had to take her fair share of unglamorous jobs while waiting for her big break to come along, including working as a receptionist and cold-calling salesperson. All the time she trudged between auditions and tried her hardest to keep the faith. She won parts in television shows and a TV-movie called *Camp Cucamonga* – 'the zaniest, most hilarious summer vacation ever', or so the billing claimed – in a comedy called *Molloy* and then on *Ferris Bueller*, which was the small-screen spin-off of the big-screen hit movie *Ferris Bueller's Day Off*.

Three weeks after the latter show screened, Aniston did her only television interview alongside her father. She remembered that he had once told her, 'If you want to make money, be a doctor.' Speaking of her own career she said, 'I can try and learn from my failures.' It was a wise motto for her to live by and she would need to be philosophical when *Ferris Bueller* flopped and was cancelled after just thirteen episodes.

It was during the filming of *Ferris Bueller* that she first dated a co-star, her diminutive fellow cast member Charlie Schlatter, though the relationship was brief. Aniston went on to receive an increasing amount of acting work in the second half of 1990 and was just beginning to fulfil the expectations of her half brother John Melick, who said, 'I guess she was destined for television.' It was an impressive prediction, because unlike many famous women, Aniston had shown few signs of achieving a future in showbusiness when she was a child. Yet here she was, making headway on the stage and small screen. A highly ambitious young woman, Aniston always wanted more, so when her agent suggested that if she wanted to progress she should lose some weight, she listened. It was tough advice, but not unreasonable as she had developed a liking for watching television and stuffing herself with mayonnaise on white bread. Given such calorific snacks, a weight increase was inevitable, though it hadn't troubled her father. 'Greeks like to eat,' he had shrugged, proudly adding, 'Jennifer was built like an Aniston.'

Once her diet saw her shed the pounds – as many as thirty according to some accounts – the job offers increased accordingly. She won a part in the horror film *Leprechaun* in October 1991, playing the part of a spoiled girl indulged by her rich father. In a sense it was similar to the television role that would later catapult her to global stardom. However, on its release in 1993 the film was slammed by the critics and only made $8.5 million at the box office. It's a film she's tried to distance herself from since, and at the time the increasingly demoralized Aniston considered giving up acting altogether. However, a man she had recently met at a party was about to give her exactly the opportunity she craved. Matthew Perry was then an unknown actor, trying hard to work his way up Hollywood's greasy pole, but when he and Aniston met, the pair clicked and became friends. It was an amusing evening, not least because a dog bit Perry in the buttocks (ironically the dog's name was Brad). In the aftermath of the *Leprechaun* disappointment, Aniston was working on a few television comedies, including Fox Television's *The Edge*. Then one day in 1994 the phone rang and Perry told her he was involved in auditions for a new television sitcom called *Six of One*. Aniston's life was about to change forever. Not that she knew it at the time.

The cast of the sitcom was to comprise six coffee-sipping singletons – three women and three men – following their lives and friendships in Manhattan. Only one of the parts was yet to be cast and there was stiff competition for the role from actresses who went on to find considerable fame in the future, such as Elizabeth Berkley and Téa Leoni. When Aniston auditioned she quickly impressed with her performance. All those TV sitcoms she had taken part in had helped hone her inherent comic ability and turn her into an irresistible prospect. Just two hours after she left the audition her phone rang. It was the producer telling her he wanted her to be Rachel Green, a fashion-obsessed and rather spoiled character.

The cast was complete, but the name of the show was to change, first to *Friends Like Us*, then to just *Friends*. The crew quickly noted the astonishing natural rapport between the six cast members. 'The chemistry was great,' said writer David Crane. 'They seemed like people who *were* friends.' Before each shoot the six would form a huddle so they felt bonded before they went to work. They filmed the pilot in the summer of 1994, but still nobody had a clue how big the show would become, especially after some damning early reviews. The *New York Times* had decided to follow the creation of the show from pitch meetings to casting to broadcast, so it had a relatively high profile in the States before the series even aired.

Once the show was broadcast it quickly became a hit with the critics, viewers and at awards ceremonies, where it went on to win sixty-three Emmys during its glorious fifteen-year, ten-series run of 236 memorable episodes. The characters – alongside Rachel were Monica, Phoebe, Joey, Ross and Chandler – added catchphrases to a generation's vocabulary and the merchandizing arm of the series became a phenomenon in itself. The final episode drew a huge 8.6 million viewers in the UK alone.

Long before the end of the show, Aniston was netting $100,000 per episode, a figure that would rise in time. Aniston adjusted with difficulty to her newfound fame. Thanks to the popularity of *Friends*, she had gone from being at best a moderately well-known actress to star and then superstar in little over a year.

In 1996, she was given an enormous shock when she settled down to watch her mother appear on a television talk show. She was expecting Nancy to discuss acting methods, but instead the interview as broadcast was almost entirely about her daughter. Aniston was livid, considering her mother's chat a betrayal, and she phoned her to make her feelings plain. Nancy tried to protest that she had been misled by the interviewers and that most of the interview when filmed was not about Jennifer, but to no avail. Mother and daughter stopped speaking at this stage, and Aniston's hurt was multiplied when, three years later, Nancy published a 278-page memoir cashing in on her daughter's fame. It was entitled *From Mother and Daughter to Friends* and was described as 'appallingly self-serving' by *Vanity Fair* magazine. Aniston told the same publication that her mother 'didn't know where she ended and I began'.

The book's revelations about herself, which were almost all innocuous, did not upset Aniston, but the dismissive remarks made about her friends did. Despite her superstardom, Aniston remained a grounded woman who was uncomfortable with many aspects of the attention she received, and when she felt that her friends were suffering she was hurt. As far as her relationship with her mother was concerned, the book was the final nail in the coffin. Nancy continues to speak of her hurt over their estrangement or, in the eyes of the more cynical, continues to cash in on her daughter's success, which far eclipses anything she achieved in her own acting career. During her publicity campaign for the book, Nancy was a ubiquitous media presence. Recalling the evening of her daughter's fuming phone call, she said, 'The one thing I'd feared had happened. I'd lost my daughter. In an instant, my life was reduced to an irrelevance.' She had to get used to learning the latest news about her daughter from celebrity magazines, just like the rest of the world did. In the years to come, Aniston would have to face a similar experience, hearing often upsetting news about her famous ex-husband through the pages of the gossip journals.

In the mid-1990s, Aniston started to date another famous figure, Adam Duritz, lead singer of the rock band Counting Crows. With his dreadlocked hairstyle he cut an iconic figure and one that contrasted with Aniston's more homely image, so perhaps it's unsurprising that the relationship fizzled out in months. Soon after they broke up, Aniston found a new man, actor Tate Donovan. The star of Fox sitcom *Partners* and the voice of Disney character *Hercules*, Donovan met Aniston in the autumn of 1995 when she was relaxing in a bar with friends. He too had recently come out of a relationship – with actress Sandra Bullock to whom he was engaged for a while. At first he didn't recognize Aniston, despite her new-found fame thanks to *Friends*. Donovan had never watched the show, but was quickly enamoured by its star, and she in turn was impressed with the six-foot actor who describes his quirky ways as akin to a 'goofball'. They began to date but broke up very quickly, due mainly to Donovan feeling uncomfortable with the media attention they received – he had, after all, had plenty of that while dating Bullock.

Three weeks after the split, however, the couple were back together again. 'He's so real, so honest, so funny, so kind and considerate,' Aniston said. 'He's all these things meshed into one perfect guy.' Whenever their schedules allowed they would spend long weekends together in her Manhattan apartment and things quickly became serious. By the time they reached their first anniversary together, the couple had exchanged Irish commitment rings and Donovan had bought Aniston a gorgeous nine-week-old puppy. He presented it to her with a red ribbon around its neck and they called it Enzo. Aniston seemed happy in this warm romance. Might a marriage be on the cards? 'There's nothing to report,' she insisted. 'You have to take more time to get to know someone.' However, she added, 'I have always been somebody that really wants to be married.' As for Donovan, he was keen as well, and hinted at the way things might develop in somewhat more emphatic terms. 'I definitely want to get married; she definitely wants to get married. There are no proposals or anything, not yet, but we definitely think about it.'

The press fascination over their relationship was huge. With *Friends* becoming an enormous worldwide hit, Aniston was famous enough in her own right to attract constant attention, but still she had a love-hate relationship with fame. The former emotion was obviously at work when – to the surprise of many – she posed naked for the cover of *Rolling Stone* magazine. No one was more shocked by the global success of *Friends* than Aniston – even Prince Charles spoke fondly of the show when he met her at a function. 'I thought, Whoa! I never figured this would be happening to me at this age!' she said of the success of *Friends*. 'I thought I would be older, wiser, better.' Add in a famous boyfriend and the recipe for regular intrusion was complete, as she was increasingly learning. 'When somebody follows you twenty blocks to the pharmacy, where they watch you buy toilet paper, you know life has changed,' she sniffed. 'I guess we can't do anything now', she added, 'without someone being there to know what we're doing.' There were plenty of happy times for her and Donovan, though. She was happy to be dating someone who, in contrast to some of her previous lovers, was not a 'bastard'. He even popped up with a cameo role in *Friends*.

Meanwhile, Aniston's movie career was beginning to blossom as she starred alongside Edward Burns and Cameron Diaz in the film *She's the One*, followed by the rom-com *The Object of my Affection* alongside Paul Rudd. There was no doubt that Aniston was the object of Donovan's affection, and people were beginning to wonder whether she was 'the one' for him.

Despite rumours that the couple had got engaged, they split in 1998. Donovan has since revealed that even when he appeared in *Friends* they were already squabbling. (She would later invite another lover – Brad Pitt – to guest star on the show.) 'Our split didn't happen suddenly,' he said, 'it was in the cards for a while.' Aniston refuted suggestions that the drawn-out split was due to a disagreement over whether or not to have babies.

Once more, Aniston had found herself unlucky in love. On the face of it she had so much: she played a popular character in one of the world's most loved television shows and had the bank balance to prove it. She had won an Emmy, a Golden Globe and a Screen Actors Guild Award for her performances. She had the looks and figure to die for, even her layered, bobbed hairstyle became the must-have hairdo of the day. 'It's bizarre,' a surprised Aniston told *People* magazine as her hairstyle was keenly replicated across the globe. More than anything, though, Aniston had a public image as a wholesome girl next door, so when Donovan attempted, following their split, to paint her as someone obsessed with 'top-notch hotels and luxury', in contrast to his own preference for 'B&Bs and riding my bike', the public refused to buy it. Her *Friends* character might have been spoilt, at least in the early episodes of the series, but nobody thought Aniston was. When Aniston later hinted that career envy on her ex's part had been a contributory factor, that rang true for many observers, but surely it only told part of the story. Donovan's father, J. Timothy Donovan, was miffed over what really prompted the split. 'Sons don't always tell their parents why they broke up,' he said. 'Jennifer and Tate are both nice people, but nice people don't always get married and live happily ever after.' His description of her as 'nice' was far more in keeping with the public's perception of Aniston. Indeed, when co-star Lisa Kudrow described Aniston's down-to-earth and selfless nature – 'No matter what's going on, her ear is always tuned into you' – that was the Aniston the public knew and loved.

As a consequence of all of this, the public didn't follow Aniston's love life with the sort of jealous fascination with which most celebrities are gazed at – people seemed to really wish her well. If anyone in the public eye deserved to find true love and happiness, it seemed, it was Aniston. So when, soon after her split with Donovan, she began to date the handsome heart-throb Brad Pitt, their relationship seemed destined to become the most popular and talked-about for some time. It was a promising and strong love from the very start. Finally, Aniston's love life was mirroring the success of her professional life. Two of Hollywood's most wholesome personalities had found love – what could possibly get in the way of all this happiness?

3. Angelina: the Other Woman

Like Aniston, Angelina Jolie was born to acting parents and faced the heartache of watching them split at a very tender age. Beyond that, the two women are and always have been very different characters. Jolie's well-known father, Jon Voight, found fame via his role alongside Dustin Hoffman in 1969's *Midnight Cowboy*, having struggled to make it in the movie industry for nine long years. They had been testing times, during which one theatre critic wrote that Voight could 'neither walk nor talk'. Still he persevered, though, and in 1962 he married a fellow cast member – Lauri Peters – from a subsequent play. The couple divorced and a few years later he met the beautiful young actress Marcheline Bertrand at a Hollywood bash. 'Jon was absolutely smitten with her,' recalled a friend. 'She was drop-dead gorgeous and heads would always turn when she entered the room.' They married in 1971, and in the spring of 1973 they had their first child, a boy named James Haven, more commonly known as Jamie. By this stage Marcheline had given up her acting career to live the domestic life. Two years after John came a baby daughter, who they named Angelina Jolie. A Gemini, she was, according to the beliefs of astrology, destined to become a woman full of energy, curiosity and with a wide variety of passions, but suffering from a shallow image.

Years later, in true Los Angeles-speak, Voight described for Jolie the moment of her birth. 'You don't remember it, but when you emerged from your mother's womb, I picked you up, held you in my hand, and looked at your face,' he said. 'You had your finger by the side of your cheek, and you looked very, very wise, like my old best friend. I started to tell you how your mom and I were so happy to have you here, and that we were going to take great care of you and watch for all those signs of who you were and how we could help you achieve all that wonderful potential God gave you. I made that pledge and everybody in the room started crying.' Within a year of making this tearful delivery-room pledge, Voight and his wife had separated. All Voight would confirm was that he 'was having difficulty with the marriage. I had an affair, and there was a divorce'. It was a divorce that hurt both children deeply.

How Jolie's relationship with her father developed following the split is the subject of strongly contrasting accounts. Jolie has often described their relationship as virtually non-existent, painting Voight as a neglectful father. 'My mom raised me,' she said, adding that 'my father and I were never close'. Later she returned to the theme, saying of her father's post-divorce role, 'He wasn't there.' However, on other occasions Jolie has given a very different account. 'I never remember a time when I needed my father and he wasn't there,' she said in 2001, warmly praising his parenting skills during an awards ceremony acceptance speech. The truth appears to lie in the latter sentiments. A nursery teacher of Jolie's remembers Voight regularly collected the children and attended school events such as sports days, like most parents did. 'He was always around,' recalled the teacher, while other sources have testified that Voight continued having a paternal role in the wake of his marriage break-up.

Part of that involved Voight giving his daughter her first big-screen role. Ironically, as she and her brother grew up it was James who was the movie buff, having to more or less drag his little sister to the cinema with him. However, it was Jolie who was the first to appear in a movie when, at the age of six, she was given a small part as a girl named Tosh in the film *Looking to Get Out*. Voight had to wave goodbye to his daughter not long afterwards when his ex-wife moved to the East Coast of America, taking her children with her to a new home near Manhattan.

It was at this stage that Jolie's behaviour became more unconventional and increasingly darker. In Los Angeles she had done nothing stranger than play with her pet snake and lizard and engage in kiss-chase games at nursery. But after encountering the streets and avenues of Manhattan, with all their contrasts, cultures and extremes, she developed some more rebellious pursuits. 'I had really gotten into leather,' she said, including collars with studs on them, and she also dyed her hair jet black, though this was only a hint of what lay around the corner.

Jolie developed an ambition to become a vampire, and sketched drawings on her school pencil case of screaming faces covered in barbed wire. Following the death of her maternal grandfather when Jolie was nine, she took on an even more macabre obsession, deciding her role in life was to become a funeral director. She began to wear all-black outfits and could be seen lurking and prowling in graveyards. She even read books about embalming and mortuary procedures. 'There is something in death that is so comforting,' she has since concluded. 'The thought that you could die tomorrow frees you to appreciate life now.' Her father watched this with some concern, telling her 'Just be pretty, hold your head up, be proud. Be a pleasant person and don't cover yourself so much with all your darkness.'

In 1986 her mother moved herself and the kids back to Los Angeles, settling in an apartment in Beverly Hills. The girl who returned to the West Coast was very different to the one who had left. 'As a child

I contemplated suicide a lot,' she said. 'Not because I was unhappy, but because I didn't feel useful.' And as she entered her difficult teenage years, these morbid, unhappy feelings intensified.

It's astounding to reflect that Jolie, whose looks are so envied today, was teased as an adolescent about her appearance. She was very thin, wore glasses and had braces on her teeth, while her fulsome lips, now considered an enviable strong point, became the target of playground bullies at Beverly Hills High School. While her classmates bought expensive clothes from trendy stores, she shopped for second-hand bargains at charity stores. This was not because her family lacked funds – although her father's pickiness over which movie offers he took up meant their cash flow was never as healthy as it could have been – but because she was aiming for a more alternative look. 'I was always that punk in school,' she said. Meanwhile Jolie was becoming more and more fascinated by fame. She tried to get some modelling work at one point, but was told by the agent that she was 'too short, too scarred, too fat, too everything'.

The scars came as a result of Jolie's obsession with knives and self-harming. 'Some people go shopping, I cut myself,' she explained. It wasn't long before this pursuit spilled over into her somewhat precocious love life. She lost her virginity at fourteen to a boy of sixteen, and their passionate romps were unconventional at times. 'In a moment of wanting something honest, I grabbed a knife and cut my boyfriend – and he cut me,' she said. 'We had this exchange of something and we were covered in blood and my heart was racing and it was something dangerous. Life suddenly felt more honest than whatever this 'sex' was supposed to be. It felt so primitive and honest, but then I had to deal with not telling my mother, hiding things, wearing gauze bandages to school.' One scar from these dangerous sessions is still visible today on her jaw line. Inevitably, this behaviour eventually got out of hand. One night she cut into the skin on her arm, neck and stomach; she began to pass out after coming close to rupturing her jugular vein and was dramatically rushed to hospital. She was subsequently ordered to see the school therapist three times a week, but wasn't impressed by the sessions, remembering: 'The doctor was probably going on about my father and my mother while I was doing acid and bleeding under my clothes.'

Jolie was also becoming increasingly inclined towards showbusiness and began taking classes at the Lee Strasberg Theatre & Film Institute. It was a good place to learn, since method-acting disciple Strasberg had tutored plenty of Hollywood royalty, including Al Pacino, Jane Fonda and Robert De Niro. Jolie quit after two years, but her subsequent pronouncements on the acting craft suggest that Strasberg's philosophies remain with her. She would also learn at the feet of her famous father. 'She'd come over to my house and we'd run through a play together, performing various parts,' he said. 'I saw that she had real talent. She loved acting. So I did my best to encourage her, to coach her and to share my best advice with her.' She appeared in a few school stage productions and, at sixteen, was able to leave previous rejections behind and start a successful career in modelling. Jolie signed up with the Finesse Model Management agency and got work in New York, Los Angeles and London. Times were good.

With her confidence on the rise after some dark and doubtful years, Jolie appeared in some student films made by her brother, who was studying cinema at university. She was on a roll and also developed a sideline appearing in rock music videos. She can be spotted in the videos for a host of tracks, including 'Anybody Seen My Baby' by the Rolling Stones and 'Rock 'n' Roll Dreams Come Through' by Meatloaf. Having taken a part in the theatrical comedy *Room Service* where, to the initial surprise of her father, she played a male part, she moved back to New York and took night classes in film studies at New York University. She also continued to model for a while, before giving that up because of the pressure of maintaining a perfect figure. Instead, she continued to audition for parts in films and landed a role in *Cyborg 2*, the sequel to the futuristic 1989 sci-fi film *Cyborg*. The film – set in 2074 – did not fare well, though, and many remember her part only for the glimpse it offered of her breasts. Once again Jolie was left depressed in its aftermath.

New York City can seem bright and exciting when things are going your way, but it can feel dark and lonely when they are not. Jolie sank to a new low and came close to suicide one day in a Manhattan hotel room. She even wrote a letter to the hotel maid, asking her to contact the police so they rather than the maid would discover her corpse. Jolie was no stranger to knives and self-harming, but even so she found it hard to pluck up the courage to go through with suicide. 'I didn't know if I could pull the final thing across my wrists,' she remembered. Instead she took to the streets of New York, staggering around in something of a daze. She contemplated a sleeping-pill overdose, or even hiring a hit man to kill her in order to avoid making loved ones feel guilty about her suicide. Gazing into a shop window, her mind focused on a pretty-looking kimono dressing gown and it gave her a slightly bizarre moment of clarity: were she to kill herself she would never be able to buy and wear that kimono. She returned to her hotel room and decided not to go through with the suicide. In making this decision, she set out a mission statement that she would live by from then on. 'I kind of lay there and thought, You might as well live a lot, really hard and not give a shit, because you can always walk through that door. So I started to live as if I could die any day.' It's a mission statement to which this woman of extremes remains true to this day.

Slowly but surely Jolie emerged from this low period and was given a significant boost when she won a part in the film *Hackers*. It was her biggest movie part to date and her first proper Hollywood role. Her character was one of a team of computer whizz-kids, led by Dade Murphy, who was played by Jonny Lee Miller. The handsome Englishman was already hot property at the time, and was on the brink of becoming a star with his role as Sick Boy in the iconic British film *Trainspotting*. For Jolie, however, he was hot in all senses of the word. She had been a fan of Englishmen since first visiting the country at the age of fourteen. 'That's when I discovered my problem,' she said. 'English men appear to be so reserved, but underneath they're expressive, perverse and wild. All the insane moments in my life have happened with English men.' Plenty such moments would happen when she and Miller became an item, and the new 'live a lot, really hard' Jolie would go on to share some of the details with the public.

Their relationship did not have a straightforward start, however. At first Jolie assumed (wrongly) that Miller, who had been involved with a musical theatre company in London, was gay. They got to know each other better during filming, but it wasn't until after production was finished that they became romantically involved. Miller was the instigator, and Jolie made him chase her for a while before succumbing. Indeed, he said he had to chase her 'all over North America . . . it took a while – a good few thousand miles'. They soon found they had a common liking of some rather notable bedroom activities. 'We are a couple who are into extremes,' he said, admitting that during their more adventurous moments he had sucked her blood. 'She digs that kind of thing,' he said. Jolie has since said of this period: 'I have always felt really naughty; I got involved in an S&M lifestyle.' She was often an open book about her private life at this time and became more so in the future, before becoming more reserved and even defensive in recent years.

On 28 March 1996, Jolie and Miller quietly, and on the face of it impulsively, got married. The only people present at the brief civil ceremony were their chosen witnesses: her mother Marcheline and his best friend, the then relatively unknown British actor Jude Law. The happy couple didn't reveal their marriage to the public until a fortnight later, when they were in Britain promoting *Hackers*. 'No, we didn't have a big white wedding,' she said, 'we had a small black wedding.' She continued to elaborate, offering information that would cement her oddball image in the public eye. She said that he wore black leather and she wore black rubber trousers and a white shirt, on the back of which she'd written 'Jonny' in blood. 'It's your husband, you're about to marry him,' she shrugged when asked about this, 'you can sacrifice a little to make it really special . . . Some people write poetry, others give themselves a little cut.' Miller, seemingly aware that this was going to make for sensational headlines, tried to temper the drama by denying that it had been 'some kind of Satanic ceremony'. Such a denial served only to put more ideas into the heads of the public as it became clear that this was no ordinary love affair.

Nor was it an enduring one, either. At this stage in their respective careers, Miller was a far bigger star than his wife. Having already lived in the shadow of her famous father, Jolie wasn't comfortable taking second billing to her husband as well. Indeed, the very nature of marriage seemed to grate with her. 'You kind of lose your identity,' she said. 'You're suddenly somebody's wife, and you're like, "Oh, I'm half of a couple now. I've lost me."' Within months of their impulsive wedding, Jolie hinted that the relationship was doomed during press interviews. 'Even if we divorce,' she said when the relationship was not yet a year old, 'I would have been married to somebody I really loved and known what it was to be a wife for a few years.' The most significant contribution that Miller and his relationship with Jolie marked was an end to her use of illegal drugs. 'I have done just about every drug possible,' she once told an interviewer. 'Cocaine, heroin, ecstasy, LSD . . . Those drugs can be dangerous. I know friends who are no longer happy or interesting, living for junk all the time and using people.' Miller, who had graphically portrayed the consequences of drug addiction in *Trainspotting*, at least helped guide her to a more sober clean-living path.

Meanwhile, Jolie's parents tried to guide her career to new heights. With her mother acting as her de facto manager and her father using his Hollywood clout to open doors, the undoubtedly talented Jolie certainly had an edge in the cut-throat movie industry. She starred with David Duchovny in the thriller *Playing God* and also took a part in the road movie *Mojave Moon*.

Jenny Shimizu was her Japanese-American co-star in the high-school movie *Foxfire*, and the moment they met, Jolie fell for her charms. 'I wanted to kiss and touch her,' she said. 'I noticed her sweater and the way her pants fit, and I thought, My God! I was getting incredibly strong sexual feelings. It never crossed my mind that one day I was going to experiment with a woman.' Shimizu, too, spoke of their magnetism, telling the *Sun* of the 'intense emotions' the couple had for one another. More memorable was her description of Jolie's mouth. '[It] is amazing, I've never kissed anyone with a bigger mouth than Angelina. It's like two water beds. It's like this big, kind of warm, mushy, beautiful thing,' she said. It seemed to be a sentiment many men shared too as a 2004 Sky Movies survey rated Jolie's lips the ones most men wanted to kiss. Stories of the fiery same-sex fling only served to add to the public's fascination with Jolie, and it also underlines the contrast between Jolie and Aniston, who at this point was riding high on the success of *Friends* while enjoying a whiter-than-white public image.

Distinctly cooler and less mushy than the passion between Jolie and Shimizu were the critical verdicts for the movie they co-starred in when it was released in August 1996. 'Probably the kindest thing to do with [*Foxfire*] would be to burn all existing prints, thereby saving everyone concerned further embarrassment,' was the conclusion of the *Atlanta Journal-Constitution*. But even though the film was panned, Jolie came out well, with *The New York Times* purring about her face being 'beautiful enough to stop traffic', while the *Kansas City Star* said she 'has a face the camera loves and seems a likely candidate for full-fledged stardom'. These words were small comfort for Jolie, who again sank into a mood of despair and considered quitting the industry in the aftermath of the film's release.

The part that saved her in the end was that of Cornelia Wallace in the television mini-series about politician George Wallace. Once again she was singled out for praise, and her performance earned her nominations for both an Emmy and a Golden Globe. She didn't win the Emmy, but she grabbed the Golden Globe for best supporting actress.

Jolie was in tears as she delivered her acceptance speech, thanking the cast and crew of *George Wallace* and the Hollywood Foreign Press Association (which makes the nominations for the Golden Globes). She then thanked her mother, brother and father and triumphantly raised the trophy, like a victorious sporting athlete. A year later she won another Golden Globe for her portrayal of Gia Carangi, the lesbian model who died of Aids at the age of twenty-six. The parallels between Jolie and Carangi were uncomfortable. Both had modelled, enjoyed same-sex relationships and taken drugs. Carangi caught Aids from using an infected needle to inject heroin. 'Playing her meant confronting a lot of things that I understand hurt me,' said Jolie. 'So it was very difficult, but it was also this great kind of purging of all that was going on inside me.' She was at pains to clarify, though, that her drug use was never on the scale of Carangi's, and explained that she had replaced her drug use with a new obsession in life: her career. After she won the Golden Globe for her performance in *Gia* she jumped into the swimming pool of the Beverly Hilton hotel in celebration, wearing a hand-beaded $3,000 Randolph Duke gown. She had jumped into the same pool as a child and been thrown out by the hotel manager. Nobody was going to tick off the famous and triumphant actress for repeating the prank this time.

Jolie and Miller had since parted ways. No single factor was cited for the split, but several obvious causes spring to mind. Jolie's friendship with Shimizu; their conflicting work schedules and Miller's claim that he was missing England: 'the nine o'clock news, red buses, country smells, the sound of our rock music, and *Match of the Day*'. Jolie was decidedly contrite after the split, admitting 'it's just that I wasn't being a wife', and adding that '[Miller] had to put up with a lot'. Their marriage had lasted only a year. Partly because of the break-up Jolie again found herself full of despair. 'I don't think I was ever more depressed in my life,' she said. Miller appeared the more upset by the split in the immediate aftermath, though he did admit that Jolie's revelations about their S&M love life did no harm whatsoever to his image. Only in time did it dawn on Jolie what a mistake she had made in breaking up with him. 'Divorcing Jonny was probably the dumbest thing I've ever done,' she has since said.

The next man she fell for was another of her co-stars: Timothy Hutton, who she appeared alongside in *Playing God*. There was a fifteen-year age gap between Jolie and her new man, who won an Academy Award when Jolie was only five years old. Indeed, early photographs of the couple showed a striking contrast in their age and attractiveness. No wonder he smiled so broadly. Despite the age gap, the pair had plenty in common as they discussed their backgrounds. Both had actor parents who split when they were children and both had moved around a lot during their childhood years. Indeed, after the wild relationships and flings of her past, Jolie had, in Hutton, found a partner who provided a more stable, calm way of life. She even had the letter 'H' tattooed on her left wrist, in honour of her new man's surname, though she later claimed it was in reference to her brother, James Haven.

By this time tattoos had become a major pursuit for Jolie. She got her first while with Miller, having the word 'courage' inked on to her while he had 'death' tattooed on him. In time she added lots more, including a dragon on her upper left arm; a Tennessee Williams quote ('A prayer for the wild at heart, kept in cages') on her left wrist; a cross on her hip; a Latin motto just above her bikini line ('what nourishes me also destroys me') and a blue rectangle above her buttocks, which she referred to as her 'window'. Heavily tattooed celebrities are more common nowadays, with stars like David Beckham and Robbie Williams regularly adding to their inkings, but Jolie was at the forefront of this trend and, as a woman, it seemed all the more shocking. She delighted in discussing her tattoos with the media and even gave them a guided tour, once again encouraging a slightly unstable media image. Not that they all lapped it up: a writer who profiled her for *Esquire* magazine said he was surprised to find that she was actually 'mushy and really close to her mom and has poetry books and lace nightgowns and wants to be cool and learn French'.

In her professional life, Jolie was being given increasingly high-profile and satisfying roles, notably with the 1999 crime thriller *The Bone Collector*. Here she portrayed a young police officer – Amelia Donaghy – alongside the legendary Denzel Washington. 'I begged for the part,' she said, and she faced a lot of resistance from the production company, but secured the part when Washington himself was impressed by her. She recognized this vote of confidence as the honour it was, particularly considering the stiff competition she faced from other actresses.

Even stiffer competition was on the cards for the part of Lisa in *Girl, Interrupted*, the Colombia Pictures adaptation of Susanna Kaysen's bestselling and harrowing memoir. A galaxy of stars, including Kate Hudson, Reese Witherspoon, Katie Holmes and singer

Alanis Morissette, lined up to try for the part, so when Jolie won the much-coveted role it was a significant moment for her. No more would film bosses ask 'Angelina who?' when she read for films. The filmmakers had been hoping for 'a kind of female De Niro' and they decided Jolie was that person, also describing her as 'a female James Dean for our time', drawing a parallel between her and Pitt.

The part she was destined to play – that of Lisa Rowe – had, like Jolie herself, been a self-harmer. To research the part, Jolie visited a bookshop and asked a sales assistant where their books on sociopaths were kept. 'Look under the heading "serial maniac",' came the reply, offering Jolie a blunt appraisal of how people like her character can be considered by society.

Jolie played the part to perfection and drew considerable praise for her performance. 'All of my characters are me,' she answered when asked how closely she related to the role. On the topic of her co-star Winona Ryder, Jolie joked, 'Ask Winona about the night we slept together.' Given her track record of getting romantic with cast members, both male and female, the joke went down well, and she had by this time split from Hutton. She then went on to joke to *Playboy* magazine that she would be willing to sleep with female fans, to the horror of her public relations handlers, who were unused to a leading Hollywood star being so upfront about her sexuality. Jolie was, rightly or wrongly, getting a reputation as a predatory lover, and the next set of rumours about her love life would be truly sensational.

At the 2000 Academy Awards ceremony, Jolie arrived with her brother Jamie, looking divine in a silky black Versace gown. When she was announced as the winner in the Best Supporting Actress category, the auditorium erupted with approval. With tears in her eyes, Jolie leaned over and kissed him, but both the length and execution of the kiss appeared more affectionate than a brother and sister would normally share. Eyebrows were raised by some audience members, and even more so during her acceptance speech. 'I'm in shock, and I'm so in love with my brother right now,' she said near the start, concluding with, 'Jamie, I have nothing without you, you're just the strongest, most amazing man I've ever known and I love you, and thank you so much.' The media and internet were awash with speculation about the nature of both the kiss and the 'love' that Jolie spoke so passionately of. Jolie protested that there was nothing inappropriate going on, and that she and her brother were simply very close after enduring their parents' divorce. Jamie also spoke out against the rumours, saying, 'Everyone who has jumped to this very sick thought is going to have egg on their face.'

Speculation carried on regardless. 'Angelina Jolie's

declaration of love for her brother was just a little too creepy for comfort,' said the *Richmond Times Dispatch*, while the Toronto *Globe and Mail* added, '"Ewww!" viewers everywhere.' Television shows also discussed it, including *The Howard Stern Show* and also *The Early Show* on CBS. It was pointed out that at the Golden Globes two months earlier, the siblings had seemed rather touchy feely, but both Jolie and her brother were quick to deny any suggestion of a sexual relationship between them. Some media outlets attempted to calm down the lurid speculation. 'Does that relationship seem a little strange?' wrote Sandy Banks in the *Los Angeles Times*, before arguing that the controversy said more about the public's prurient cynicism than it did about Jolie and her brother. In retrospect the incident seems a little contrived, and given Jolie's love of manipulating the media at the time, perhaps it was feminist cultural commentator Camille Paglia who came closest to the truth when she wrote, 'I think Angelina was messing with people's heads.' If this was a pre-planned publicity stunt then it was to prove harsh on her brother, who found the resultant media storm very difficult to deal with. He got upset by the attention and jokes, and Jolie felt that keenly, admitting, 'It's put a distance between us.'

The man she was definitely getting physical with at this stage was actor Billy Bob Thornton. Indeed, he was the first person she contacted after her Oscar night success, as the world was feverishly discussing her kiss with Jamie. They had first met in 1998, on the set of the movie *Pushing Tin*. Their then joint manager, Geyer Kosinski, had long thought the two would hit it off if they met, telling Thornton that Jolie was 'the female you'. And when they did meet, Thornton described the feeling as 'like a bolt of lightning', while Jolie spoke of an almost 'chemical' reaction. Their relationship did not get serious, though, until 2000, and in May of that year, Jolie spent seventy-two hours in the UCLA Medical Center after checking herself in. She was devastated at the thought that her and Thornton might never become an item and complained of 'paralysing grief', driving her to further thoughts of suicide. As she told *Rolling Stone* magazine, 'I just went a little insane.' Her mother contacted Thornton and within days he and Jolie were not only an item, but married. The wedding took place in Las Vegas and cost just $189. Jolie wore a blue sleeveless jumper and jeans, while Thornton was equally casually attired, finishing his outfit off with a baseball cap.

The service on 5 May 2000 was just twenty minutes long and was the 'Beginning Package' option in the Little Church of the West wedding chapel in Las Vegas. 'They came in like anyone else,' remembered the chapel owner Greg Smith. Jolie strolled down the aisle to the sound of 'Here Comes The Bride', carrying red and white roses, and they altered the vows so Jolie promised to love and honour her husband, but not obey him. None of her family were present at the ceremony, which brought together two slightly peculiar characters to make the most bizarre couple in showbusiness. In an industry where the images of celebrities are carefully managed by their advisers, you couldn't have found two people who were more plain-speaking, early-disclosing and downright indiscreet. Together they made a pair that would keep the headline writers busy for some time. Thornton described how they would 'stalk each other round the house' and, speaking of their love-making, said, 'Every time we do it, it gets more and more exciting.' Jolie complained that she had rug burns after the couple had sex on a pool table at home. 'He does certain things to me in bed that, well, they're beautiful.' When they spoke to reporters on the red carpet at the MTV Awards later that year, Thornton told one, 'We just fucked in the car.'

As they continued to describe their passion for one another, the disclosures got more amd more detailed and disturbing. 'I was looking at her asleep and literally had to restrain myself from squeezing her to death,' said Thornton, who had denied claims by his fourth wife that he had physically abused her. Angelina subsequently responded, 'You know when you love someone so much you can almost kill them? I nearly was killed one night, and it's the nicest thing anyone's ever said to me.' They set up home – buying a property from Guns 'N' Roses guitar legend Slash in keeping with their wild ways – and bought two pets, a rat called Harry – coincidentally also the name of one of Thornton's sons from a previous relationship – which they kept in a cage at the end of their bed, and a talking myna bird called Alice, which Thornton attempted to teach to say 'fuck you'. Their pets were so central to their life that when the couple renewed their wedding vows they even worked references to the creatures into their vows. Even more strangely, during the ceremony they cut their fingers and sucked one another's blood.

Jolie and Thornton also famously took to wearing vials of each other's blood around their necks. As ever, Jolie was willing to spill the details to the media, and it's not entirely clear how many of the stories involving her and Thornton's behaviour are true. However, some of her statements to the press made for shocking reading. 'Some people think a diamond is really pretty.' She shrugged. 'My husband's blood is the most beautiful thing in the world to me . . . If there was a safe way to drink his blood, I would. He's my soul.' Thornton had also taken to wearing her knickers when she was away working, in order to feel closer to her. More and more revelations emerged from their camp, such as the fact that Jolie had written, in her own blood, 'Till The End Of Time' on a plaque, which she placed above their bed. As they celebrated their first anniversary together, Thornton wrote the same words underneath in his own blood. She later handed him a box containing her blood and informed him she had purchased his-and-hers cemetery plots for them in Arkansas. Thornton wondered what he could do to upstage these astonishing and ghoulish gifts. 'I guess I'm just going to have to fly up to the moon, tear it in half and hand her a piece,' he said. When Jolie subsequently tried to make a more conventional gift for her husband, her attempt to knit a scarf went wrong and she abandoned the project.

Jolie's next professional project was to appear as the lead in the action movie *Lara Croft: Tomb Raider*, a film based on the top-selling computer game. On the face of it, the action-packed role seemed a surprising one for Jolie, particularly after starring in the more cerebral *Girl, Interrupted*. Commercially, though, it was a great and strangely suitable part: the computer-game character Croft sleeps with knives, and Jolie for one argued that she was perfectly cast. 'I'm very loud and physical and insane,' she said, 'so I fit this role perfectly. The strange thing is that she actually looks like me. Our skin, our hair and our bodies are just the same.' Not exactly: to play the curvy, muscular daredevil Croft, Jolie had to alter her lifestyle considerably. 'From the time I got up in the morning I had to drink a certain amount of water, had protein checks with food experts, ate egg whites and took vitamins, and all the bad things in my life were taken away.' She rose early each morning to do yoga and took on a number of physical pursuits, including kick-boxing and bungee ballet. Having been a size 36C, she went up to a D cup for filming but to achieve Croft's full busty look she also had to pad her bra. Jolie also had to speak with a posh English accent when in character and, despite a few lapses, managed well. The film was an enormous success and she drew hearty praise for her part.

The most significant legacy of her involvement, however, was of a more life-changing nature. Some of the filming took place in Cambodia, and Jolie's experiences there were to leave a lasting impression on her. She described the country as 'the most beautiful place I've ever been', and the people of Cambodia made their mark on her too as she described them as 'so generous and open, kind and spiritual'. The effects of the civil war were still very evident, and Jolie was disgusted to learn that children were still being routinely killed by land mines. Just like Diana, Princess of Wales it was a fact that haunted her, as she encountered, she recalled, the 'horrifying depths of human suffering'. On her return to the States she retained a desire to help the people she had seen and contacted the United Nations High Commission for Refugees (UNHCR), who sent her on goodwill, awareness-raising trips to Tanzania and Sierra Leone. Her experiences there would have been harrowing for anyone, but for a cosseted Hollywood star they were particularly eye-opening.

Jolie also met Afghan refugees in Pakistan, where she witnessed the harrowing sight of little children scrambling through rubbish looking for food, and in the summer of 2001 she was appointed UN Goodwill Ambassador. After the September 11 attacks on New York and Washington shook America and the world, her connection with the people of the Middle East became controversial, particularly when she spoke of her concern for the people of Afghanistan in the wake of the attacks. Some Americans were less than impressed with her sentiments and she even received death threats.

During her travels to deprived, embattled parts of the world, Jolie tried to spend as much time as possible in the frontline among ordinary people, taking care to dress humbly, removing any jewellery and expensive items. 'I didn't want to flash anything of value,' said Jolie, 'not because I feared theft, but because I felt so bad.' On her flight back from Africa she didn't want to remove the jacket that had got so dirty during her visit, feeling that to do so would be a disrespectful break from the people she had grown so attached to. It felt strange enough to have left them living in the squalor of the African jungle to board a first-class flight back to America. 'My impressions are hard to cope with, so I write them down,' she said, heralding the publication of *Notes From My Travels*, a journal about her trips. The next outcome of her goodwill role was to alter the story of the Hollywood wild child forever and bring her a more mature and balanced image. It was not mere window-dressing, though. This was a genuine sea change in her life, and behind the scenes she was about to take an even more profound step.

On 11 March 2002, Jon Voight was lunching with some fellow actors when he told them, 'I'm a grandfather today'. Jolie would be angry when she found out he had revealed the news before she'd wanted it known, but it was indeed true. She had often hinted that she would like to have children with Thornton one day, to add to the two sons he already had from his previous marriage. She told *E! News* that she had gone off the idea of becoming pregnant and would adopt instead, but since both she and Thornton had a self-confessed history of mental health issues and drug use, domestic adoption would be difficult. Consequently she began to look overseas, as she first told Larry King on CNN. 'Ever since I can remember, after hearing about different kids that need homes or . . . orphans,' she told the presenter, 'I've just always known that I would love [an adopted child] as much as I would love my own.'

Given her love of Cambodia, her concern for the children there and her desire to adopt, there was a sense of inevitability about what happened next. Since Cambodia had relaxed criteria for adoption, it made sense for Jolie to look there, but at the time, news of her visit to an orphanage in Battambang, near the Cambodia/Thailand border, was a big surprise. She was in the orphanage for two hours. 'I decided I'd not go for the cutest child but just go to the one that connected to me,' she said. She saw a sleeping baby boy who, when he woke up, smiled at her. The three-month-old boy was called Rath Vibol and it was he who Jolie selected. She admitted later that she'd had momentary doubts about her suitability for the role. 'They put him in my arms and I stared at him and I started crying and he smiled. I hadn't held children before in my life. I was always considered so dark and I thought maybe I shouldn't be someone's mum because I'm not so sure about myself – am I going to be the best mum?' She added, 'The fact that this little kid seemed so at ease gave me the courage to feel I could make him happy and so we became a family.' She renamed him Maddox Chivan and then had to wait several months for the various legal and administrative procedures to be completed.

At the end of April 2002 she was free to bring Maddox to America to start their new life together as mother and son.

Yet amidst the joy of starting a new family, there was also heartache. The headlines were being simultaneously taken up with news of her split from Thornton. 'He's never been to a refugee camp,' she told *US Weekly* magazine. 'I asked him to come, but he chose not to. You learn what a person is about by their behaviour. And sometimes what they do hurts you.' She explained that the last time she had seen Thornton was the day before her twenty-seventh birthday and that they'd had an 'ugly' argument. The coverage of their split not only overshadowed the controversy over the details of her adoption of Maddox, she also emerged from the relationship as the caring, compassionate woman, while Thornton was painted as a cold character who'd hurt her. As one Hollywood publicist noted, she began her relationship with Thornton while facing difficult headlines about her relationship with her brother, and ended it when facing difficult headlines about her adoption.

The appearance of Maddox in Jolie and Thornton's lives seems to have been the catalyst for the split. Given that Thornton has used the words 'selfish' and 'insecure' to describe himself, it's not hard to imagine how difficult he would have found it when his wife's attentions became centred on a child rather than him. He reportedly phoned Jolie regularly, begging her to allow him back into her life, but she was adamant. There could be no going back. She took down the 'Till The End Of Time' plaque that had stood above their marital bed and placed it in the household's fireplace. She then visited a tattoo remover and endured a number of laser treatments to have 'Billy Bob' removed from her left arm. 'I'll never get a man's name tattooed on my body again,' she said in the wake of one painful session. As for Thornton, he chose a slightly different path, having his 'Angelina' tattoo shortened simply to 'Angel'. When she parted with Miller, Jolie spoke glowingly of her ex-husband and their time together, but her statements about Thornton were less upbeat. She even admitted, 'I'm beginning to accept I'm terrible at marriage.'

But how did she rate herself as a mother? She said she was 'loving being a mom' and explained how, in an experience that many mothers might find surprising, she was feeling 'more beautiful these days . . . I think I look my most beautiful when I'm rocking my son to sleep, it's the middle of the night, I'm exhausted and I'm covered in his dinner'. As she changed nappies, standing in well-worn sweatpants, without time even to shave her legs, she found that she felt 'more of a woman' for the experience. She also didn't feel that their lack of a genetic link gave them less of a connection; rather, Jolie felt that it made their relationship more sincere. 'He doesn't have to love me,' she said of Maddox. 'And I don't have to love him, because we weren't forced together by blood . . . If he grows up and really accepts me as a mom it's because I've earned it and not because he has to.' With her relationship with Maddox so strong, she wasn't in a rush to start a new relationship with a man, even though she was keen for her adopted son to have strong male influences. She was keen to avoid 'Mad', as she sometimes called him, getting close to a man who might subsequently disappear from his life, and she was also wary of men who might dote over her son only because they saw it as a fast route to her affections.

In the wake of the split, Jolie reportedly pulled off a public relations masterstroke when a leading magazine approached her to try and secure an exclusive interview and photo shoot. Jolie wasn't interested in such a deal and politely declined to take part. However, according to a report in *The New York Times*, Jolie then suggested a different idea to the magazine. She allegedly tipped them off about a time and location when she and Maddox would be out in public, sharing a personal moment together as mother and son. The magazine accordingly took photographs of them at the given time and place and published them without explaining to the readers that these images – which appeared as unsolicited paparazzi shots – had actually been co-ordinated by Jolie and the publication. 'She's scary smart,' said Bonnie Fuller, a former editor of *Us Weekly* and *Star* magazines. 'But smart only takes you so far. She also has an amazing knack, perhaps more than any other star, for knowing how to shape a public image.'

In a way, art imitated life when Jolie took a part in a film about aid workers called *Beyond Borders*, playing Sarah Jordan alongside British star Clive Owen. It was Owen who explained just how motivated Jolie was to take part in the film due to its promotion of humanitarian work. 'She was very passionate about doing the film,' he said. 'It wasn't a vanity thing of what a fantastic part it was. It was: I want to point people towards this subject.' Away from work, Jolie was enjoying probably the most grounded and serene time of her life since her childhood. That calm was shattered, however, in October 2003 when she was warned her son might be the target of a kidnapping by Chechen terrorists. She had been planning a trip to Chechnya with the United Nations to meet with refugees. 'I was told not to bring my son because extremists might try to hurt him,' she said. This would not be the last time she would face the terrifying prospect of one of her children being kidnapped. Jolie's travels to dangerous parts of the world were causing concern for some of those closest to her, including her father who, when he decided to speak out, did so very publicly.

For some time, their relationship had been tested. One day, as they parted, he handed her a letter saying, 'This is my truth.' According to Jolie, the contents of the letter painted her as 'a bad person'. She was hurt, as were her mother and brother when they saw the letter, so she decided to sever all connections with her father. When he approached her at a Los Angeles bash, her handlers blocked his way, explaining that she didn't want to see him. Her father subsequently showed up at the Dorchester Hotel in London, hoping to see her, but so eager was she to avoid him that she rushed into the back seat of a taxi and ordered it to speed away, even leaving her luggage on the pavement. Voight was devastated by these rejections and believed it wasn't his daughter behind them, but those around her. 'When the money train is running, everybody wants to be on it,' he said. He was about to make their private dramas public, but if he believed that was the way to win back her trust and affection, he was sadly mistaken.

On 2 August 2002, an emotional and at times tearful Voight appeared on the popular American television programme *Access Hollywood*, speaking about his ruined relationship with his daughter and his concerns for her. 'I don't know what else to do,' he said. 'I'm broken-hearted because I've been trying to reach my daughter and get her help and I have failed. I'm sorry, really. I haven't come forward and addressed the serious mental problems she has spoken about so candidly to the press over the years. But I've tried behind the scenes in every way. I've seen Angie in tremendous pain. She carries tremendous pain. I've seen that pain in her face.' With tears running down his face, he continued, 'They're very serious symptoms of a real problem . . . real illness. I don't want to look back and say I didn't do everything I could.' For Jolie, the hurt at seeing a parent discuss personal matters on television must have been similar to how Aniston felt when her mother did the same thing. Like Aniston, Jolie decided to end the relationship and said that while she felt sorry for her father, he was now 'not any more to me than a man who walks down the street'. She had long ago dropped 'Voight' from her name, but she now chose to make that change official by legally removing it. Jolie's mother came publicly to her defence, telling *People* magazine, 'There's nothing wrong with Angelina's mental health. Mentally and physically, she is magnificently healthy.'

In the wake of Voight's interview, Jolie chose once more to paint him as a bad father. She told reporters that they 'were never close' and profiles of her began to routinely say that Voight had 'abandoned' his family when he and her mother divorced. Entirely absent from the story was the fact that he had remained a close and attentive father during Jolie's childhood. Almost nowhere to be seen were mentions of the recent fun times they had enjoyed, as Voight encouraged his daughter in her acting career, offering her tips and opening doors for her. Long forgotten were the words of Jolie herself who, in her Oscar acceptance speech in March 2000, had said, 'Dad, you're a great actor, but you're a better father.' Once more Jolie spun the media the way it suited her at the time, and Voight was left feeling hurt and facing difficult headlines, just as Haven had after the controversial kiss he and his sister publicly shared. Perhaps the final word on the truth about Voight's fathering skills should go to neither him nor Jolie. Instead, let's reflect on the words of Jolie's mother, who told *People* magazine, 'Nothing means more to Jon than the children.'

Having removed, and in some cases replaced, some of her tattoos in recent years – including the one she'd had done in honour of her now ended marriage with Thornton – Jolie had a spectacular new one applied in August 2003, this time in honour of her son Maddox. On her left shoulder, where she had once had 'death' written in Japanese, she had a Buddhist Thai prayer of protection for her son applied.

She said that the Thai artist who inked the new tattoo used a 'foot-and-a-half-long needle'.

Maddox proved to be as much of an individual as his mother when he was sent to a posh school in their new home in England. Sporting a mohican-style haircut, he also wore jewellery, including a helicopter necklace. Although Jolie's longstanding love affair with England remained as strong as ever, she was not impressed with the school's conservative approach to attire. 'They downplay the individual, which is a problem,' she sighed in an echo of the statements she had previously made about her uneasiness with some aspects of marriage.

While she was in England she also spent time with her ex-husband Jonny Lee Miller, and the couple were spotted kissing in public and getting new tattoos together. However, if there was a rekindling of their love, it was not to last.

On the big screen, Jolie continued to work hard. In 2003 she starred in the sequel *Lara Croft Tomb Raider: The Cradle of Life*. Other roles she took at this time were the voice of Lola in the hit animation *Shark Tale*, and Olympias in *Alexander*, the epic story of Alexander the Great, directed by Oliver Stone. Soon after that she was cast in *Mr. & Mrs. Smith*, in which she would play Jane Smith, the wife of John, who was to be played by Brad Pitt. Her co-star was dropped off at the set by his wife Jennifer Aniston, and as she waved her husband off, Aniston told Jolie, 'Brad is so excited about working with you. I hope you guys have a really good time.' They are words that assume a haunting quality in the light of what happened next.

4. Brad and Jen: the Perfect Couple

Just two months after Jolie married Billy Bob Thornton, another celebrity couple tied the knot. In contrast to Jolie and Thornton's low-key, bargain-basement ceremony, theirs was an extravagant affair costing over a million dollars, attended by a huge cast and followed by a global audience. Security was tight around the wedding, which took place on beautiful Malibu beach and caused part of the busy Pacific Coast Highway to be closed so that events could run as smoothly and privately as possible.

At the end of the evening, as the happy couple watched the $20,000 firework display that capped off their wedding day, they will no doubt have reflected on their love and perhaps remembered how they'd first got together two years earlier. The way they met marked something of a departure for Pitt, whose previous girlfriends had mostly been co-stars. When he filmed *Dallas* he dated Shalane McCall; his *Head of the Class* co-star Robin Givens was also a love interest for a while; then came his relationship with Jill Schoelen, who he met on the set of *Cutting Class*. He also reportedly dated – with varying degrees of seriousness – other co-stars, including Juliette Lewis, Genna Davis, Thandie Newton and Julia Ormond. His relationship with Aniston might have come to an end after he became close to another co-star, but it did not begin on the set of a film or television show.

Although they had met briefly in 1994, Pitt and Aniston's first public outing was not until March 1998, when they had an evening meal that was reportedly arranged by their respective agents (not an uncommon way for Hollywood couples to meet). The evening went well, and a few days later Pitt left a phone message for Aniston, who was preparing to visit England to film the *Friends* season four finale, 'The One With Ross's Wedding', suggesting they meet again. Perhaps she would like him to pop round and help her pack? As Aniston later told Oprah Winfrey, 'I was so nervous I never called him back. When I got back from England we had a date. I fell in love on our first date.'

Here were two people destined for a special connection, their common ground going far beyond the fact that they were both Hollywood actors. In an industry full of debauchery and an undignified hunger for fame, Brad and Jennifer had long been considered exemplary characters. Furthermore, both had the mixed blessing of extraordinary good looks. But though they benefitted from their beauty, both were tired of being recognized for their looks ahead of their acting ability. Their first two dates were such a success that they were soon socializing at his pad in Los Feliz and her small house on Blue Jay Way, overlooking the celebrated Sunset Boulevard.

Jennifer recalled to *Vanity Fair* magazine how they 'huddled' on the sofa. They loved watching television – both were fans of English soap opera *EastEnders* – and enjoyed smoking. Pitt was mightily impressed that Aniston smoked cigars, a pastime Telly Savalas had introduced her to. They ordered in takeaway food, including steak and mashed potatoes, and Aniston's dog Norman was the first of those close to her to give Pitt his approval. 'It was like a little love nest,' Aniston recalled fondly. Very soon she decided that this was a love that was 'very much meant to be'. When she flew to Texas for the filming of her new movie, *Office Space*, Pitt travelled with her and they stayed at the Four Seasons Hotel. They were later spotted cuddling backstage at a rock concert in Washington. They still didn't make their relationship official publicly, however, giving evasive answers to the increasingly curious media. On the evening of the premiere of Pitt's latest film, *Meet Joe Black*, they arrived separately and banned the media from the after-show party. Behind the scenes, the relationship was flourishing, though, with Aniston's friends noting approvingly that she was very much herself around her new man.

In 1999, Pitt invited 500 of Aniston's friends to a party in honour of her thirtieth birthday. It was held at Sunset Boulevard's hip Barfly restaurant and was a fun-packed evening that saw them become even closer and fonder of one another. Then, on 11 February, the day of Aniston's birthday itself, the couple and nine close friends flew by private jet to Acapulco in Mexico. They remained there for Valentine's Day three days later, enjoying a cosy dinner before dancing until late in the evening. Even during these happy times, though, there were stark reminders of the costs of fame. As they romanced in Mexico, Pitt's home in Los Feliz, Los Angeles, was broken into by a stalker, who was later placed on probation for three years and ordered to undergo psychiatric treatment. She was reportedly wearing Pitt's clothes when she was discovered. Then Aniston was unwittingly photographed sunbathing topless in her garden. Despite having posed nude for *Rolling Stone* magazine in the past, she considered this invasion of privacy to be in quite a different league, and was furious when the photographs were subsequently published in America and Europe. Pitt was equally angry, having suffered from a similar photographic intrusion when he and Paltrow were dating.

In the face of such regular and intrusive media interest, the couple knew they could not keep their relationship secret for much longer. In September

A young Brad Pitt and the two women who would become the major loves of his life: Jennifer Aniston and Angelina Jolie.

Brad's incredible physique was always clear to see, but it was only when he was cast as 'J. D.' in Ridley Scott's blockbuster film *Thelma and Louise* that his magical combination of acting talent and raw sex appeal reached a global audience.

The chemistry shared between Brad and his co-stars has often led from the film set to the bedroom . . . *Top left*, Brad poses with Shalane McCall, who played his onscreen girlfriend in the TV series *Dallas*, while *top right*, Brad poses with another of his major flames, the talented actress Juliette Lewis, with whom he starred in *Too Young to Die?* and *Kalifornia*. However, it wasn't until he met Gwyneth Paltrow on the set of the 1995 film *Se7en* and fell in love that the previously commitment-shy Brad first gathered the nerves to 'pop the question'.

He was to propose four times before she agreed to marry him.

Angelina Jolie, possibly one of the most beautiful women ever to grace the earth, was perhaps destined to become a star of the screen. The daughter of two talented actors, Jon Voight and Marcheline Bertrand, acting was always in her blood.

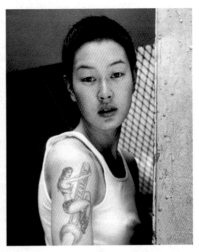

Like Brad, Angelina's love affairs have often developed from onscreen partnerships. Her first marriage to British actor Jonny Lee Miller in 1996 came on the back of *Hackers*, the 1995 film in which they both starred. In the same year they married, Angelina starred in *Foxfire* with Jenny Shimizu, with whom she began a sexual relationship. Jolie was later to say, 'I fell in love with her the first second I saw her.'

Challenging boundaries and expectations has always been in Angelina's nature, from sharing a shockingly intense red-carpet kiss with her brother, James Haven (*pictured with Angelina, right*), or admitting to risqué sexual antics with her second husband, Billy Bob Thornton, with whom she starred in 1999's *Pushing Tin*.

When Brad started dating *Friends* actress Jennifer Aniston, following a blind date, it seemed like a match made in heaven – the Hollywood hunk and everyone's favourite girl next door. And in the first flush of romance, the pair seemed to have found a heaven in each other's arms.

Above, Brad appeared in a brief cameo role in *Friends*, much to the delight of fans worldwide. *Left*, the couple at a post-Oscars® party in 2000.

Whether caught unawares out for a walk or snapped on the red carpet, Brad and Jen seemed to have a relaxed way with each other that many assumed spelt a lifetime together.

1999 they made their first official outing as a couple to the Emmy Awards at the Shrine Auditorium in Los Angeles. They had both clearly given a lot of thought to their appearance and looked sensational. Jennifer went for a slightly messy, braid-ridden blonde hairstyle, while Pitt was in fine physical form after the intense training he had undertaken to film the movie *Fight Club*. He had blond highlights in his hair – which were compared to a recent look sported by football ace David Beckham – and a neat goatee beard. A month later he arrived at the *Fight Club* premiere hand in hand with Aniston, who was relieved to be able to declare their love to the world. 'Brad's the cutest guy on earth, and he's so deep and spiritual,' she told reporters. 'I love being in his arms, I want to have his baby.'

During the summer of 1999 Aniston showed that, like Jolie, she had a compassionate and charitable nature. However, in contrast to Jolie's high-profile roving ambassador role, Aniston's work was more discreet: volunteering at a rape treatment centre in Santa Monica. 'It's too easy to call out these charities you're part of,' she said. 'So many people want to stand up for something, but it can be dangerous. We have a voice, but you have to educate yourself first. Truthfully, I would do it all if I could, but I've just been finding things I'm moved by.' Aniston's charity work often goes on behind the scenes, but is not un-noted by those who benefit, nor by other famous activists, such as feminist actress Kathy Najimy who said, 'You name it, she's done it.'

In November 1999 it emerged that Pitt had proposed to Aniston, who had quickly said yes. They then made an unexpected and peculiar on-stage appearance alongside Sting at the Beacon Theatre in New York. Jennifer was the first to emerge, during the song 'Fill Her Up', and was joined onstage by Pitt, who held up her hand to reveal to the audience the engagement ring he had given her. Soon afterwards they paraded their bliss at the *Vanity Fair* post-Oscars party, drawing admiring glances wherever they went. The stage was set for the most glamorous wedding of the millennium to date.

The day before their wedding, Aniston admitted to feeling apprehensive. 'I had those typical jitters,' she said. Given the scale of the event and the amount of planning that had gone into it, she could be excused feeling nervous. Security, which was arranged by a former Mossad agent, was tight. As well as the sealing off of part of the highway, security guards armed with machine guns prowled the borders of the estate where the wedding was taking place. Reports suggested that all staff were asked to sign a confidentiality agreement, which threatened a six-figure fine if they leaked details to the press. Even the 200 guests were kept in the dark about the event's final details, being asked only to report to Malibu High School and await transport to the venue itself. When they arrived, they were greeted by a vision of paradise. There were over 50,000 flowers, including lotus flowers floating in a beautiful fountain, and nearly as many lanterns and candles – some imported from Thailand, as requested by Aniston, and a forty-strong gospel choir who sang 'Love Is The Greatest Thing' before the ceremony.

Aniston walked down the bridal walkway holding her father's arm. She was wearing a $52,000 long, silk backless dress, complete with tiny pearls, designed by Lawrence Steele. Her veil and tiara were also dotted with pearls and crystals, and she completed the stunning outfit with four-inch Manolo Blahnik ivory sandals. As she joined Pitt, clad in a Hedi Slimane dinner jacket, at the altar, their matching blond-streaked hair made them seem even more suited. The bridesmaids wore Lawrence Steele green silk tunics and the flower girls wore cream silk. The best man was Brad's Prada-clad brother Doug, who inadvertently lightened the mood when he dropped the ring. The rings had been designed especially by Pitt and were diamond-embedded white gold, with 'Brad 2000' and 'Jennifer 2000' inscribed on them. Jennifer slipped up during her vows, but turned the mistake into a virtue by joking, 'Sorry, but I've never done this before.' The couple had written their own vows for the day and these too were riddled with comedy.

Jennifer vowed to keep making him his banana milkshake, while he vowed to 'split the difference on the thermostat'.

After the ceremony they cut the six-tier wedding cake, locking eyes as they did so, and when they took their first bite, they laughed uproariously with sheer glee. The music for the party was extravagant and exciting. Guests danced to a bouzouki band and smashed plates in the great Greek tradition, and there was a child crooner present to sing the popular love song 'The Way You Look Tonight'. Then it was time for a special, acoustic performance of Led Zeppelin's 'Whole Lotta Love', sung by their old friend Melissa Etheridge, with actor Dermot Mulroney on mandolin. Finally came that spectacular firework display, which went on for thirteen breathtaking minutes. 'They wanted it big, grandiose, the greatest effects that we had,' explained a representative of the pyrotechnics company they commissioned for the job. During the display some of Pitt's favourite songs – by Radiohead, Garbage and Jeff Buckley – were played, capping off an extraordinary evening.

The guest list on the big day included all of Aniston's co-stars from *Friends*, with the exception of Matt LeBlanc who was filming in Hungary. Other stars present included Sir Anthony Hopkins, Morgan Freeman, Bruce Willis, Madonna, Guy Ritchie, Cameron Diaz and Edward Norton. Matthew Perry said the evening was the most romantic of his life, and the joy of the day was topped by the fact that the paparazzi didn't try to infiltrate the event. 'And I have to really thank them because they were just so cool,' Pitt later told Jay Leno. 'They let us have our moment, they let us have what turned out to be the highlight of my life.' As those present testified, although it was a grand day, it was also a grounded one. 'It was an emotional service,' said one guest. 'It wasn't like a business thing. It was friends and family and celebration.' There was one family member missing though: Aniston's mother was not invited to the wedding since she was still paying the price for publicizing details of her daughter's life. Aniston had slightly eased the tension between them by publicly declaring her mother as 'warm, loving, nurturing, wise, funny and old-fashioned', but relations weren't good enough for her to be included in the couple's big day.

All in all it was a blissful day, cementing the stature of Pitt and Aniston as Hollywood's golden couple. The global interest in their relationship elevated the marriage to that of a royal wedding. The only question was, could they live up to the fairytale image the world had bestowed upon them?

During the first year of their marriage, there were occasional hints that the fairytale might be headed for a heartbreaking early finish. 'This has been the hardest part of my life, as well as the best year of my life,' Aniston told *Vanity Fair* nine months into their marriage. 'The period after the wedding was extremely intense for lots of reasons.' The interview was a cocktail of paranoia, self-doubt and other dark emotions. Although these weren't explicitly linked to her marriage, the expression of such feelings so early on in married life didn't bode well. It took the couple time to move into their first marital home, forcing them to live in hotels for long periods. Then there was the fact that their work schedules often forced them apart. 'Distance is a beast,' said Pitt, who chatted with Aniston via primitive webcams whenever his schedule allowed. He flew around Europe and Morocco to film the thriller *Spy Game*, and while Aniston joined him during breaks in filming *Friends*, the journeys became hard for her due to a growing fear of flying.

In addition to this, the media began to gently chip at their wholesome image by claiming they were enthusiastic dope smokers. Pitt has never confirmed or denied the rumour, but Aniston told *Your Life!*, 'I enjoy it every once in a while'. There were also whisperings in the media that Pitt was disappointed in Aniston for not communicating with her mother. Certainly Pitt has always been close to his own family, so the reports that a 'friend' of the couple claimed they'd had 'big fights' about the matter has a ring of truth to it.

Whatever was going on behind the scenes, however, both their careers were thriving. In a precursor to the monstrously profitable 'Brangelina' brand, Pitt and Aniston found that their American sweethearts union was decidedly bankable, and that together they were worth far more than they were apart. Aniston was now receiving a quarter of a million dollars for each episode of *Friends*, earning her a total of $18 million per season. Meanwhile, Pitt was starring in huge movies, including *Ocean's Eleven* alongside George Clooney, who, when he observed the couple together, described them as very 'homely'.

At last, the 'homely' couple were buying a house together, having purchased a $14 million, 10,000-square-foot, six-bedroom property. It was a grand house that had once belonged to 1940s film star Fredric March, who won Oscars for his parts in *Dr Jekyll and Mr Hyde* and *The Best Years of Our Lives*. Even when the purchase was completed, however, matters were not simple and the renovations dragged on for two years. This delay coincided with difficult times for the couple. When she made the film *Bruce Almighty*, Aniston was asked by a journalist what she would do if granted godly powers and she answered, 'I would have the house finished.' The couple were by this time living in Aniston's original house, but when it flooded they had to move again, to a new temporary place in the Hollywood hills.

The women who for years had watched *Friends* from their sofas had loved seeing Aniston marry her showbusiness Prince Charming, not just because they were pleased for their heroine, but because it offered hope that they too could net their own dreamboat. Consequently there were cheers galore when happier noises emerged from the couple's camp and they took some well-earned time off together to enjoy married life properly. When they spent Valentine's Day 2001 apart, Pitt arranged for Aniston's dressing room to be filled with a thousand roses, with petals arranged on the wall to spell out, 'Your husband loves you.' When Valentines 2002 came round they spent it together at posh sushi bar Katana on Sunset Boulevard, where Pitt raised a glass to his wife, saying, 'You're my best friend, my soul mate, the one I'll spend eternity with.'

Such nights were romantic and fun, the very stuff of a successful marriage, but perhaps the warmest glow came from the ordinary days they spent at home. They would listen to music, read, watch television and simply enjoy being with one another. Pitt taught his wife to play the guitar, they ordered in takeaway meals and followed the drama of television reality show *Survivor*, on which they were hooked. Sometimes they'd invite chums over and play table tennis, dominoes or charades. 'We're so boring,' Aniston told *O*, Oprah Winfrey's magazine. To live such a happy and straightforward life with a handsome hunk like Pitt sounded anything but boring to most female observers. Not that they didn't make public appearances. Photographs of them at the premiere of *The Good Girl* in 2002 show them happy and relaxed in each other's company, with Pitt sporting a shaggy beard not unlike the one he grew in 2010. He was growing it in preparation for his part in *The Fountain*, a film he did not in the end take part in.

Could this domestic bliss become yet more blissful with the addition of some children? In May 2001, Aniston said that she hoped to have two or three children with her husband, but that Pitt wanted seven kids. The remark seemed to be intended humorously, with Aniston adding that he'd need a mail-order bride to fulfil that total, but it is true that Pitt had his heart set on a large family. Brad had already shown signs of his paternal urges by inviting kids from neighbouring houses round to play football with him. These were popular kick-abouts that showed how natural he was with children, but still there was no word of him fathering his own.

Increasingly, their public statements and behaviour suggested that all was not well with their relationship. Aniston was asked by *W* magazine if Pitt was the love of her life and replied that she wasn't sure, but 'he's certainly a big love of my life'. She also referred to arguments in the household, admitting, 'We do fight.' When she arrived to collect a People's Choice Award at the Pasadena Civic Auditorium, she came alone, the seat next to her remaining empty, while her husband was also absent – filming in Malta – when she attended the marriage of *Friends* co-star Matt LeBlanc. Pitt did accompany his wife to the Golden Globes ceremony, but the couple arrived late. It should have been a joyful event, as she'd won the award for Best Actress in a Comedy Series for *Friends*, but it was given a dark tinge. First she was forced to limp on stage because of a broken toe, then she forgot to thank her husband during her acceptance speech. He was caught on camera as his previously happy, proud expression turned to one of disappointment when he realized he wasn't going to be mentioned.

When the couple moved – finally – into their marital home in July 2003, Pitt was again away filming, this time in Mexico for the film *Troy*. Aniston cut a lonely figure as she performed the important and symbolic move from her old house – which rather than sell she had rented out to British star Sacha Baron Cohen – to the new house they'd spent more than a year, incalculable effort and $1 million renovating. Indeed, the renovation issue had been a fraught one for the couple as Pitt – a modernist – has strong opinions on architecture and design, opinions that Aniston, who is more of a traditionalist, does not share. Aniston had particularly focused on the room that was destined to be the nursery, strongly supervising the work on this part of the mansion. Pitt told an Australian newspaper that the couple's minds were very much focused on parenthood, saying his preference was for girls rather than boys. 'There's no question about it. I love girls. I want little versions of Jennifer. That's my dream.' The issue of children was to take on an increased, and hotly contested, significance after the pair split.

The media became awash with speculation over when Aniston would become pregnant, so much so that she ended up asking a *Vogue* reporter, 'Do you all want to be there when we conceive?' She had grown frustrated with the relentless speculation over whether she had given up smoking because she was already pregnant. News that she was taking daily doses of folic acid – a supplement often taken by women when trying to conceive – only fanned the flames. One rumour suggested that towards the end of filming *Friends*, Aniston had been in the early stages of pregnancy and had suffered a miscarriage, then in the summer of 2004 a story circulated that Aniston was pregnant, with news channel MSNBC saying an unnamed 'inside source' had confirmed the story. Officially, Aniston's spokesman neither confirmed nor denied the report. When she signed up – against her husband's wishes – for a tenth season of *Friends*, and then signed up to appear in films to be made after *Friends* had wrapped, that particular story faded away.

The questions about when, or even whether, she planned to become a mother did not, however. Diane Sawyer, anchor of ABC's *Primetime Live*, asked her about it in early 2004. She replied that she would 'definitely love to have two', and added, 'This'll be probably the most important job I'll ever do, having a baby.' An earlier remark from Aniston, made during an interview with *Cosmopolitan* in 1997, also bears repeating, for it shows that her desire to have children was strong and long-running. 'I love everything about [babies],' she said, 'their backs, necks, smell, all their fits,' adding, 'I want to be a young mom, too.'

Despite the cracks that some commentators were identifying in the golden couple's marriage, there were plenty of positive signs for those with a mind to look for them. Aniston told how they saw an elderly couple out driving together and watched as the man lovingly touched the woman's hand. 'He seemed to say, "I've loved you for 7,000 years, and I still do,"' she told a magazine interviewer. 'I hope that's Brad and me one day.' Pitt, too, made warm noises, saying, 'Marriage is great. It's made me feel very good about taking this kind of journey together with a terrific woman who wants to share my life and share the journey with me.' It certainly seemed at this stage that their love and marriage was forever, and the public, who remained enthralled by movie land's golden couple, hoped so too.

However, trouble was just around the corner and their 'great' marriage was, in fact, doomed from the minute Aniston dropped her husband off on the set of *Mr. & Mrs. Smith*, offering the aforementioned friendly well-wishes to his co-star Angelina Jolie: 'I hope you guys have a really great time.' What prophetic words they were, though not in the way Aniston would have wanted.

A crew member later claimed in *US Weekly* magazine that Pitt and Jolie 'both went after each other' more or less as soon as work started on the film, though both parties deny that anything physical happened at this stage. 'It wasn't like she was just after him and seducing him,' continued the quoted source. 'They wanted each other. It was pretty obvious.'

So what did happen on set? And why did Pitt and Aniston's seemingly idyllic marriage fall apart?

5. Mr and Mrs Smith: the Rumours and the Reality

Whether deserved or not, Jolie had earned a reputation as something of a seductress long before sparks flew between herself and Pitt. When she and Thornton began dating three years earlier it was widely perceived that she had pinched him from fiancée Laura Dern, so reports of extreme behaviour between her and Thornton, and her subsequent ditching of him, did little to remedy her damaged public standing. Jolie has always been obsessed with her image and how she can work publicly and behind the scenes to improve it, and her humanitarian tours of war-torn countries had certainly earned her a more sympathetic hearing. Now, however, growing suggestions that she was having a fling with Brad Pitt, one half of Hollywood's golden couple, and husband of the enormously popular and wholesome Jennifer Aniston, threatened to wreck her image irrevocably. Whatever the truth behind their relationship, the public would naturally be more disposed to sympathize with the down-to-earth, everywoman Aniston than the wild and seemingly predatory Jolie, with her colourful background and straight-talking ways.

Mr. & Mrs. Smith is an entertaining romantic comedy with an espionage-themed twist that's reminiscent of a film made twenty years earlier, *Prizzi's Honour*, starring Jack Nicholson. Both members of the titular married couple discover they are assassins who have been hired by rival agencies to murder each other, and the part of Mrs Smith almost went to Nicole Kidman before falling to Jolie. Ironically, rumours at the time suggested that Aniston had been unhappy at the thought of her husband being on set with the recently single Kidman, whose marriage to Tom Cruise had just ended. Catherine Zeta-Jones was also in the frame before Jolie took the part and travelled to begin production in Los Angeles.

As sparks reportedly flew between Pitt and Jolie behind the scenes, there were public clues that his growing fondness for her coincided with a slow erosion of the foundations of his marriage. 'I hate the notion of fairy tales,' he told *Vanity Fair* in early 2004. 'No one can live up to such a thing. Marriage is tough, it's not easy. There is so much pressure to be with someone forever and I'm not really sure if it's in our nature to be with someone for the rest of our lives.' He added that himself and Aniston 'didn't cage each other with this pressure of happily-ever-after'. While on the road promoting *Troy* in April, he still spoke in strikingly unromantic terms. 'Neither of us wants to be the spokesman for happy marriage, for coupledom,' he said of himself and his wife. 'I despise this two-becomes-one thing, where you lose that individuality.' His sentiments echo Jolie's, who complained that marriage made her feel as though she'd lost her identity, and they're a far cry from his previous statement that he was delighted Aniston, a 'terrific woman', wanted to 'share my life'. Perhaps unsurprisingly, it wasn't long before the couple started referring to each other as 'friends'.

Keen observers will have noticed that, just as Pitt began to speak dismissively about lifelong commitment, he also started to speak glowingly about his new co-star, Jolie. 'I've never seen someone so misperceived in the press,' he insisted to reporters in April. 'Jolie's a really delightful human being, a dedicated mother and really quite normal. [She's] dedicated to her work with the UN. There's actually a real lightness to her.' In return, Jolie credited Pitt with giving her the confidence to take her first comedic part in *Mr. & Mrs. Smith*. Although it's customary for Hollywood actors to speak with sickening sweetness about their co-stars, these were nonetheless the first public hints that something was afoot.

Behind the scenes there was plenty more to be suspicious of. After shooting a scene at an LA restaurant, the cast and crew of *Mr. & Mrs. Smith* retired to the Standard Hotel, a boutique establishment that's anything but standard. There was a real party atmosphere as everyone wound down with drinks and revelry on the rooftop terrace, and there were reports that the stars of the film – Pitt and Jolie – enjoyed an intimate moment during the festivities. Pitt's spokesperson, Cindy Guagenti, said, 'They have gotten close because they have been working together, but that's it.' Jolie's representatives also issued a strong statement along the same lines.

Aniston read these stories like everyone else and they tested every part of her determination not to be a suspicious or jealous wife. 'I had a period in my life when I was younger when I was jealous,' she once told an interviewer, 'but I don't feel that now.' She said of her husband, 'He's very loyal.' Aniston joined Pitt at the Cannes Film Festival in May and, according to some reports, Pitt's management suggested to Jolie's handlers that the pair might keep a low profile for a while. Even if this was true, it wouldn't stop what now seemed inevitable.

Aniston's faith in her husband's loyalty would be tested throughout 2004. Back on the set of *Mr. & Mrs. Smith*, Pitt set up a patio area outside his trailer which became known as 'Brad's Grotto'. Regularly and increasingly, he would be joined there by Jolie and her son Maddox. While a strong bond between the two cast members was undeniable, a powerful attachment was also growing between Pitt and Maddox. It seemed that Pitt – who had been very vocal about his desire to have children as soon as possible and now at forty years of age was probably feeling a sense of urgency about becoming a father – was enjoying the quasi-paternal role he had with the boy. When filming moved to Italy, Pitt was seen joyfully playing with Maddox at the Hotel Santa Caterina in Amalfi.

As suspicions grew, further denials were made. 'He is not having an affair with Angelina Jolie,' Guagenti told the media in October. Soon after, Jolie herself spoke out. 'I wouldn't sleep with a married man,' she said. 'I have enough lovers. I don't need Brad.' Soon afterwards, Pitt and Aniston dined out together in a London restaurant and Pitt announced that he was looking forward to them spending Christmas together. They did that, but were apart for Pitt's birthday on 18 December.

As if to make matters worse for Aniston, her therapist died out of the blue and she was forced to face a succession of press stories claiming that the problems in her marriage were connected to her unwillingness to start a family, in contrast to her husband's keen wishes. 'Insiders claim Pitt's desire to start a family and his wife's reluctance to give up her career have caused "intolerable pressures",' ran one newspaper report. This was followed by similar reports in the following months, in which unnamed sources were quoted as making the same suggestion. Still the suspicion and fascination mounted, and in

December Pitt turned up at the premiere of *Ocean's Twelve* alone, refusing to speak to the media as he walked up the red carpet. While promoting the movie in Tokyo he had only taken press questions he deemed 'polite', but at the LA premiere the journalists shouted their questions regardless, and nearly all of them were, 'Where's Jen?' Or even, 'Where's Angelina?' He could dodge the questions that night, but sooner or later something had to give.

After spending Christmas together, Pitt and Aniston flew to the beautiful Caribbean island of Anguilla. Alongside them were their friends (and *Friends* co-star) Courteney Cox, her husband David Arquette and their baby Coco, Aniston's goddaughter. On the face of it, the holiday had all the trappings of the ideal romantic double-date getaway. They took relaxed walks along the beach, stopping to kiss tenderly, Brad wearing a grey jumper with a 'Trash' logo on it, Aniston wearing a blue sarong. Perhaps Jolie's insistence six weeks earlier that she wasn't sleeping with Pitt was true and this holiday was the beginning of a new and happier future for the golden couple? In fact, the trip was taken so the couple could say goodbye to each other in happy surroundings. The day after they had been seen walking tenderly along the beach, Pitt's publicist Cindy Guagenti issued a carefully worded public statement that had been composed by the couple: 'We would like to announce that after seven years together we have decided to formally separate. For those who follow these sorts of things, we would like to explain that our separation is not the result of any speculations reported by the tabloids. The decision is the result of much thoughtful consideration. We happily remain committed and caring friends with great love and admiration for one another. We ask in advance for your kindness and sensitivity in the coming months.' Of course, this carefully constructed statement did nothing to quench the media thirst for detail and scandal – sensitivity would come at a premium in the coming months.

When considering the farrago of rumour and insinuation that was to follow the announcement, it's worth bearing in mind the atmosphere of co-operation and serenity that characterized the way the split was handled. This didn't appear to be a couple splitting up as a result of infidelity. The reports centred on three main theories: that they broke up after arguing over the issue of children; that they split as a result of Pitt's fondness for Maddox; or because he was having an affair with Jolie. Since Jolie was such an obvious candidate to be painted as the 'baddie' in this story, the media started building a case for her as a home-wrecker, suggesting that Pitt had cheated prior to his marriage break-up.

It is beyond dispute that Pitt was enamoured by

Jolie during the making of *Mr. & Mrs. Smith*, and it's tempting to speculate that this took on a physical edge. However, Aniston's friend Courteney Cox said that she didn't believe Pitt had a physical relationship with Jolie prior to their split, though she described an intense attraction between them. 'There was a connection and he was honest about that with Jen,' she said. 'Most of the time when [married] people are attracted to other people, they don't tell. At least he was honest about it. It was an attraction he fought for a period of time.' Another of Aniston's friends said that she was well aware that there was 'an enchantment, a friendship,' between Pitt and Jolie, and it does seem unlikely that if he had been cheating on his wife – and she was aware of it – they could have had such a moving and affectionate farewell as they did in the Caribbean. 'We exited this relationship as beautifully as we entered it,' Aniston later said.

However, the saga turned ugly in late January when a magazine published a photo shoot featuring Pitt and Jolie on the set of *Mr. & Mrs. Smith*. Their body language was intimate and in one of them they seemed very physically affectionate. True, these were two actors who were experts at playing roles, but the fact that these shots had been taken the previous autumn – before the split – fuelled suspicions that the pair had got down and dirty some time ago. These and other photographs would be unavoidable for Aniston in the future, who admitted, 'It's hard to be the abandoned one.'

So what of the suggestion that Pitt and Aniston's marriage fell apart because of his desire to start a family, and her reported unwillingness? From the day following the announcement of the split these stories kept appearing in the press. 'It's about children,' an unnamed 'friend' of the couple told the *New York Post*. 'She just doesn't want kids right now, and he wants kids.' Hot on the heels of that came another report claiming, 'A pal said Aniston doesn't want to take time off to have a kid and she doesn't want to endure the physical effects that giving birth will have on her sexy body.' Then came another uncited report saying that Aniston's 'obsession with her career' in the face of Pitt's broodiness was to blame. As Aniston read these stories with growing horror, the media photographed Pitt playing the father-figure role with Maddox on Diani beach in Kenya. As he and the boy built sandcastles together, the loving image was captured on camera and plastered all over the world's media. The contrast between the snaps of him looking proudly paternal, and the uncited reports about Aniston's alleged unwillingness to have children was strong. Fortuitously for Jolie, these photographs and reports helped to deflect suggestions that she had been having an affair with Pitt.

The lady herself had spoken to *Marie Claire* magazine in March 2005. 'To be intimate with a married man when my own father cheated on my mother is not something I could forgive,' she said. 'I could not, could not, look at myself in the morning if I did that.' To drive home her point, she added, 'I am not dating anybody. I think the next man I get involved with would have to become Mad's father, and that's a high bar as far as I'm concerned. I'm not anticipating that coming anytime soon.'

The same month as the magazine hit the streets – where it was snapped from the stands by a fascinated public – Aniston filed for divorce, bringing to an end any hopes – as expressed by, among others, Pitt's grandmother Betty Russell – that the couple might get back together and give the marriage a second try. It was an essentially straightforward and amicable divorce, legally at least. The only part that was at all complicated was the matter of the production company they had launched jointly during happier times. However, Aniston was hurt badly by the photographs she saw of Pitt and Jolie together, and as she faced more suggestions that her marriage had collapsed because she favoured her career over having children. Feeling isolated, abandoned and vilified, she seethed and cried and eventually decided it was time to have her say.

The September issue of *Vanity Fair* featured an

emotional interview with Aniston, which had been conducted in her bungalow in Malibu, not far from where she had married Pitt five years earlier. The magazine sent Leslie Bennetts to do the interview, and she remembered how, as she opened the door, Aniston burst into tears. The interview saw Aniston in animated mode as she defended herself against what she felt had been unfair and sexist coverage of the divorce. 'A man divorcing would never be accused of choosing career over children. That really pissed me off,' she said. 'I've never in my life said I didn't want to have children. I did and I do and I will! The women that inspire me are the ones who have careers and children; why would I want to limit myself? I've always wanted to have children, and I would never give up that experience for a career. I want to have it all.' She also admitted that she threw 'pity parties' for herself and would on occasion walk on to the beach and scream with sheer hurt and frustration. 'I would be a robot if I said I didn't feel moments of anger, of hurt, of embarrassment,' she added. In researching the article Bennetts also interviewed several mutual friends of Aniston and Pitt, and an image began to emerge from these chats that painted a very different picture to the one being spun by the media.

'When Brad and Jen were in the marriage, having a baby was not his priority – ever,' one friend told Bennetts. 'It was an abstract desire for him, whereas for Jen it was much more immediate. So is there a part of Brad that's diabolical? Did he think, I need to get out of this marriage, but I want to come out smelling like a rose, so I'm going to let Jen be cast as the ultra-feminist and I'm going to get cast as the poor husband who couldn't get a baby and so had to move on?' With the public already more naturally disposed towards Aniston than Pitt and Jolie, sympathy swung her way once more.

Stories emerged which painted Aniston and her supposed unwillingness to have children as the cause of the marriage's collapse. Whatever was behind these stories, *Vanity Fair* magazine was more concerned as to why Pitt didn't speak out and deny them. 'To some, this looks like sheer hypocrisy,' claimed the magazine. It wasn't until the summer of 2005 that he finally broke his silence on the matter, telling *GQ* that the whispers were 'total bullshit' and *Primetime Live* that they were 'ridiculous bullshit'. Wherever the stories had come from they were clearly untrue. They might have taken some of the heat off Jolie, but they weren't enough to knock the halo from Aniston's head in the court of public opinion, as was about to be memorably demonstrated.

Kitson is a fine designer emporium in Los Angeles. Noting the huge public fascination with the story, they produced two sets of T-shirts with rival logos: Team

Aniston and Team Jolie. Here was an immediate way for the women of America to give their verdict on the controversy. The result was that Team Aniston T-shirts outsold Team Jolie ones by twenty-five to one. It was a striking and attention-grabbing vote of confidence for Aniston, but the portrait painted by *Vanity Fair* of a tearful, frustrated but dignified woman was perhaps an even more powerful image. It was one that stood to paint Pitt and Jolie in an increasingly negative light, and both members of the couple are keenly aware of the importance of their public image.

'It was horrendous,' said Jolie of the time the tide turned against her. 'When it was happening, I simply tuned out. There was a lot of toxic stuff out there, and to be able to survive all that it was necessary to move through it as cleanly as I could and think positive.' The couple were still officially denying that they were a romantic item and preferred to present themselves merely as good friends. When they attended the premiere of *Mr. & Mrs. Smith* they arrived separately and the media were told the pair would not be willing to answer questions about the nature of their relationship.

Earlier in the day, Pitt had been interviewed on *Primetime Live* by Diane Sawyer, where he preferred to focus on his recent awareness-raising trips to poverty-stricken areas of Africa than on his personal life. However, Sawyer made sure she grilled him about his personal life as well. 'It's a really interesting time,' he said. 'It's a shake-up year. I made my choices and I live with those. I like that. My mistakes are my mistakes. My wins are my wins – that I can live with.' Sawyer brought the conversation round to his relationship with Jolie, and he replied, 'It's more that there's not so much to talk about at this time. There's a lot still to, I guess, put into place . . . Listen, I don't know what the future is yet.' It wasn't an unequivocal denial, but still the official position was that he and Jolie were not an item. When asked by Sawyer whether Jolie was the cause of the collapse of his marriage, Pitt said, 'No, it's a good story.'

A great story, as far as the media was concerned. Across the world journalists sharpened their pens and photographers and cameramen focused their lenses. Everybody wanted to get the scoop that two of Hollywood's most celebrated, successful stars of the moment were an item. However much they tried to dodge the relentless focus, the pair were still celebrities with films to promote, making it impossible to avoid the questions.

Jolie appeared on NBC's *Today* show with Ann Curry, who was formidable in her questioning, encouraging Jolie to come clean and pointing out that doing so would take the sting out of the story forever. 'People will say what they want to say, and it's OK,' said Jolie. 'And my life will go on, and I need to focus on my life. So, do I need to defend that I'm a decent woman? I sure hope I don't. I know I am.' This was an entirely different Jolie to the one who had previously made graphic boasts about her love life. Perhaps parenthood had made her more demure, but the suspicion that she had pinched Pitt from Aniston appeared to have shaken her too. Curry was not about to let the subject pass, though, and asked Jolie again about Pitt. 'I think the world of Brad,' said Jolie. 'We did eventually become close – any couple working so intimately would. But I will tell you there was no bedroom action. But, yes, my feelings for him did escalate. And love? Well, what is that? I feel love for my little boy Maddox. And, yes, I suppose a different kind of love remains between me and Brad. What I will say is that we have grown very close.'

Later that year, however, stories surfaced which suggested there was a physical side to their relationship. Newspaper reports quoted a source who had overheard the couple making love while on holiday in Africa. The description was vivid, to say the least, saying the couple's passionate noises 'sounded like a wounded animal, like someone being killed'. Indeed, claimed the report in the *New York Post*, so torturous was the noise that security at the resort were concerned the couple were being attacked by lions and knocked on their door. 'Everything is cool, guys,' Pitt reportedly assured them.

For Aniston, these were difficult stories to be made aware of. It's the sort of nightmare scenario that women dread: their man being stolen by a lustful sexual predator who offers him wilder times. She explained wryly, 'I can't say it was one of the highlights of my year, but shit happens.' Indeed it does, and in the eyes of many it happened again when Pitt and Jolie decided to participate in a photo shoot for *W* magazine. The magazine was running a sixty-page spread entitled 'Domestic Bliss'. Along with photographer Steven Klein, Pitt created a concept of a series of photographs portraying himself and Jolie as an unhappily married suburban couple living in 1960s America. They were featured as man and wife, with a gang of 'mini Brads' playing the part of their children. Pitt explained that he hoped the photographs would explore the 'unidentifiable malaise' that destroys marriages. The photographs were artistic but, under the circumstances, rather tasteless. As Aniston said of them, 'There's a sensitivity chip that's missing.'

A friend of hers – Kristin Hahn – spoke of Aniston's pain: 'This woman is basically having a root canal without anaesthesia,' she said. Gossip magazines continued to snap Pitt and Jolie as they travelled round the world together, including visits to Pakistan, Tokyo and Canada, and Aniston would find it hard to avoid the photographs which were widely published. Still, she and Pitt continued to insist that he was faithful during his marriage. 'He didn't do anything while he was married,' a source said. 'He'll go to the grave saying that.' It must have been hard for Aniston to know what to believe, and looking back she attempted both to be philosophical and to distance herself from the matter. 'Look, I'm not defined by this relationship,' she told *GQ* magazine. 'I wasn't when I was in it and I don't want to be in the aftermath of it. And that's really important to me. Let's let everybody move on and live their lives, and hopefully everybody will be really happy.' It was a magnanimous gesture and one that maintained her image as a kind soul.

Aniston takes leave from the story at this stage, but it won't be the last Pitt hears from her, nor is it the last we shall hear from her in these pages.

Two years later, in an interview with *Vogue*, Jolie finally started to open up about what had happened between herself and Pitt during the production of *Mr. & Mrs. Smith*. 'I think we were both the last two people looking for a relationship,' she said. She explained that back then she was content to be a single mother, looking after her adopted son Maddox. Although unclear at the time what Pitt was seeking from life, she said, 'It was clear he was with his best friend, someone he loves and respects.' Therefore, she said, neither of them were actively seeking a relationship together, though circumstances were to change as the filmmaking continued. 'We ended up being brought together to do all these crazy things, and I think we found this strange friendship and partnership that just kind of suddenly happened.' Slowly, she explained, their affection for one another built and she found herself excited about seeing him. 'I think a few months in I realized, "God, I can't wait to get to work." Whether it was arguing about a scene or dance class or doing stunts – anything we had to do together – we just found a lot of joy in it together. We just kind of became a pair.' Still they insisted that it wasn't until after shooting had finished that they even realized they might want something more.

'It took really until [that point] for us to realize that it might mean something more than we'd earlier allowed ourselves to believe,' she continued. 'And both knowing that the reality of that was a big thing, something that was going to take a lot of consideration. We spent a lot of time contemplating and thinking and talking about what we both wanted in life and realized we wanted very, very similar things. And then we just continued to take time. And then life developed in a way where we could be together, where it felt like something we would do, we should do.' Part of what they should do, they felt, was build a family together. Just six months after Pitt had broken up with Aniston he travelled with Jolie to Addis Ababa in Ethiopia to collect a sister – born the day after Pitt and Aniston split – for Maddox. Originally called Yemsrach, the girl was renamed Zahara Marley by Jolie. 'Maddox and I are very happy to have a new addition to our family,' she announced. A month prior to her collection of the baby, she explained how she had felt compelled to adopt a child from Africa for two reasons. Firstly she was haunted by the memory of seeing a child die in a refugee camp during a previous visit. 'I went home and I thought, "I should have at least taken one,"' she told CNN. Also, she continued, she had been influenced by Maddox, who was keen for an African sibling. This adoption was the next phase in her dream of assembling a 'rainbow family'.

Jolie had been searching for a suitable sibling for Maddox for some months. In November 2004, according to a report in the *Daily Mail*, she had been 'scouring' orphanages in Russia in search of a child of 'Slavic appearance'. She reportedly found several children that took her fancy, including a blond-haired, blue-eyed boy called Gleb. But she left empty-handed. A director of one orphanage was quoted as speaking dismissively of her visits as 'something of a circus'. Jolie has said of the trip, 'I was going to adopt this other child in Russia, but it didn't work out, so I may adopt another in about six months.' Which was roughly the stage at which she adopted Zahara. The girl was an Aids orphan, living in a basic, one-room shack with her grandmother and aunts. Sceptics suggest that Jolie gave up on the Russian route and turned to Africa because the latter option provided a less complicated adoption process. However, adopting from Africa was not without red tape, as Jolie – and Pitt, who was symbolically at her side for the trip – discovered. The couple, tired of questions about their love life from the voracious media, faced further interrogation from the adoption authorities about the nature of their relationship. 'The woman said, "How long have you been together?"' recalled Jolie. '"And can you explain your relationship?" And she's obviously not a reporter. She's just a woman doing her job.' It seemed that, one way or another, everyone on the planet had an interest in them.

Six months after the adoption, Pitt legally adopted both Zahara and Maddox, and both children's surnames were changed to Jolie-Pitt. In the case of Maddox in particular this move was a formal recognition of what had already become a father/child relationship. One day, out of the blue, recalled Jolie, Maddox had turned to Pitt and called him 'Dad'. 'It was amazing,' she told *Vogue*. 'We were playing with cars on the floor of a hotel room, and we both heard it and didn't say any- thing; we just looked at each other. And then we just kind of let it go . . . that was probably the most defin- ing moment, when he decided that we would all be a family.' Soon after arriving back in America with Zahara, Jolie encountered the sort of challenge every mother dreads. She noticed that her adopted daughter was very light for her age. 'Her skin, you could squeeze it, it stuck together,' she remembered. Luckily, the vigilant Jolie took her daughter to see a doctor, who immediately diagnosed a salmonella infection, which had led to malnutrition and dehydration. Zahara was rushed to the emergency room in the New York Presbyterian Hospital on Fort Washington Avenue. Jolie was alone as she maintained a round-the-clock bedside vigil, because Pitt was, by coincidence, in a different hospital at the time fighting off a bout of viral meningitis.

After all the controversy surrounding her adoptions and her relationship with Pitt, Jolie now had a chance to demonstrate a different side to her character. The paediatrician in charge of Zahara's recovery, Jane Aronson, spoke glowingly of Jolie's bond with her daughter, saying, 'They are one, they're in love.' Zahara was nursed to recovery and soon began to eat healthily, so much so that the much-relieved Jolie and Pitt nicknamed her 'chubby'.

Although relieved by her daughter's return to health, Jolie faced more heartache when she had to face speculation over the circumstances of Zahara's adoption. A number of women in Africa had come forward claiming to be Zahara's mother. Jolie had always said her daughter was an Aids orphan, so these reports threatened to cast question marks over the entire adoption. Then Zahara's grandmother claimed her granddaughter had been adopted against her wishes. The Ethiopian court in Addis Ababa investigated the claims and ruled that Zahara's mother had indeed died and that the father was unknown, meaning that the adoption could stand, much to Jolie's relief.

While Jolie filmed her latest movie in the Dominican Republic – a history of the CIA called *The Good Shepherd*, which was directed by and stars Robert De Niro – Pitt shot *Babel* and *The Assassination of Jesse James* elsewhere. The pair kept in constant contact, though. They had been forced to weather numerous storms recently, but finally things were beginning to stabilize in their lives. Indeed, they would soon make a public announcement about a new addition to their lives who would – joyfully – confirm their love once and for all.

Before turning to that, though, let us step aside and consider the trends and forces that saw Brad Pitt and Angelina Jolie's relationship change from an inauspicious start to become more than that of just a celebrity couple and instead reach the heights of a phenomenon – or brand – that is so much more than the sum of its parts.

6. Brangelina

Celebrity couplings clearly have a lot to recommend them to all parties with anything at stake in the fame game. For the two stars involved the advantages are plentiful and obvious: most notably the prospect of a partner who understands the pressures of living in the public eye and who has a comparably large income. While professional rivalry and envy might be a factor, at least they are both chasing the same career commodities: fame and fortune. Together they are stronger – they can increase their level of recognition, and with it their bankability is almost certain to soar. For the media these relationships are pure gold, a paparazzi dream come true, because any stories, photographs or interviews relating to celebrity relationships are lapped up by the reading and viewing public, who delight in such romances. Pitt and Jolie's relationship has taken this longstanding, mutually beneficial feeding frenzy to a whole new level, though they are far from the first celebrity couple.

In the 1920s actor Douglas Fairbanks married actress Mary Pickford, and the famous couple returned from their European honeymoon to increased fascination and adoration, as demonstrated by the cheering crowds that greeted them. The same decade saw the tragic courtship of author F. Scott Fitzgerald and his novelist wife Zelda Sayre. Just as Brangelina's romance sometimes plays out like a Hollywood movie, so the Fitzgeralds' lovelife mirrored the wonderful, weaving plots of his novels. Two decades later Humphrey Bogart's marriage to Lauren Bacall ensnared the public imagination, not only due to their age gap – Bogart was twenty-six years her senior – but because the marriage of two famous faces pressed so many buttons with the public. The elopement of baseball player Joe DiMaggio and superstar Marilyn Monroe was the talk of the 1950s and once more upped the stakes for future famous couples as the press and public became gripped by their story.

It was Burton and Taylor, though, who truly set the blueprint for the twenty-first-century 'supercouple'. Burton fell in love with the double Oscar-winning Taylor during the making of the 1963 film *Cleopatra*, and the film's director described working with them as akin to being 'locked in a cage with two tigers', such was the intensity of their passion. A year after production ended on the film, the couple wed, and they became the subject of mounting public and media interest during their ten-year marriage. The public was spellbound by the charismatic couple. These were decadent times and few were more indulgent than

Burton and his wife. They stayed in luxury hotels, attended posh banquets, shopped at the most exclusive stores, sailed on yachts and showered each other with expensive gifts – no wonder the public was enthralled by their love and lifestyle.

Paving the way for future celebrity couples also included heartache and hullabaloo, both of which they provided plentifully for a fascinated world. Taylor attempted suicide when it seemed Burton might leave her; he drunkenly shouted of his love for her across crowded restaurants and once described her as 'beautiful beyond the dreams of pornography'. The Vatican denounced the couple, memorably accusing Taylor of 'erotic vagrancy', while Burton once said of Taylor, 'If anything happened to her, I'd die.' When they divorced in 1974, the press wrote widely about the story, quoting Taylor as saying that the relationship was always doomed. 'You can't keep clapping a couple of dynamite sticks together without expecting them to blow up,' she said, using vivid and memorable imagery. However, after they split, both doubted whether they had done the right thing and remarried within a year, in Botswana of all places. A condition of their reunion was that Burton should stop drinking, but he had already broken his promise by their honeymoon, and in a flurry of headlines they finally went their separate ways only eleven months later, in the mid-1970s.

The legacy of their relationship lives on to this day

as famous couples find that together their stars shine brighter and that by forming a supercouple they become even more famous. David and Victoria Beckham were famous and successful in their own fields prior to their marriage in 1999, but have since become a phenomenally wealthy and iconic couple with global influence. Their marriage, just prior to the turn of the century, set the bar for the other stars that followed in their wake.

To be clear: two famous people in a relationship does not a supercouple make. For instance, actor Ben Affleck dated Pitt's ex-partner Gwyneth Paltrow in the late 1990s, and though their relationship kept the media gripped, it was a small story compared to his next relationship with actress/singer Jennifer Lopez. The couple's names were merged into a single word – 'Bennifer' – signifying the potency of their partnership, but when they split and Affleck subsequently married actress Jennifer Garner, the new couple didn't achieve the same status, despite her conveniently having the same first name as Ms Lopez. Similarly, although Madonna's relationships with Guy Ritchie and Sean Penn were much discussed and written about, neither of them reached the stature of supercoupledom. The next famous couple to achieve that status was actor Tom Cruise and Katie Holmes, who became an item not long before Pitt and Jolie. Cruise proposed to Holmes at the top of the Eiffel Tower and the public lapped up the story, following the birth of their first child with colossal excitement. It didn't hurt that the couple's names conveniently blended into the memorable moniker Tom-Kat.

When Pitt and Jolie officially became an item, the media were quick to brand them a supercouple, and accordingly christened their partnership 'Brangelina'. The couple intensely dislike the term and have encouraged magazines to drop it, but to say that they benefitted and profited from the nickname is an understatement. The level of interest surrounding them has reached the point of insanity, and that fever began well before they were even officially a couple. In 2005, the internet site eBay hosted an auction for a jar of air that might have been breathed by Pitt and Jolie on the set of *Mr. & Mrs. Smith*. 'Be the first to own this jar of celebrity air, which may contain air molecules that came in direct contact with Angelina Jolie and Brad Pitt,' read the seller's statement. The bidding soon reached six figures, despite the additional disclaimer which read, 'We are not guaranteeing this air sample contains air molecules that came in contact with any celebrity epidermal layer or respiratory system, but the sample was captured in proximity of the celebrities and air molecules that did come in direct contact.' It was extraordinary and there was plenty more madness to come. Even in these celebrity-fixated days of *Grazia*, *Hello!* and *Heat* magazines, it signified a new and almost desperate obsession with getting close to the glittering world of the famous.

The celebrity world has had a neat succession of top-of-the-tree supercouples since the mid-1980s. Once Prince Charles got engaged to Lady Diana Spencer in 1981 they became the media's top couple, through their marriage later that year, their divorce in 1996 and then Diana's tragic death in 1997. By that time, David Beckham and Victoria Adams' relationship was in the ascendance, and they took top billing when they married in 1999. By the mid-2000s, with rumours of infidelity surrounding the marriage, their union remained a media obsession but was ripe for replacement, which happened temporarily when singer Pete Doherty and supermodel Kate Moss's rocky relationship briefly plugged the gap.

Pitt and Jolie could scarcely have timed it better. There were media whispers that the couple were planning to marry, with the first reports emerging on Christmas Eve 2005. The high-circulation American magazine *Life & Style* claimed that Jolie was three months pregnant with Pitt's child and that the wedding was to take place on New Year's Eve. The report said that Jolie's costumes on the set of *The Good Shepherd* had to be changed because of a bump. An 'insider' told the magazine, 'People on set were thinking, she's obviously pregnant.' There was, of course, no wedding on New Year's Eve, but that day did see reports surface that the couple were planning to move permanently to Normandy in France, where it was claimed they had their eye on a fine 127-year-old mansion. Ever the jetsetters, two weeks later they made a high-profile trip to the Caribbean island of Haiti, to draw attention to the peril and poverty that many of its people face. 'You hear so much just about the danger and the fear and then you come here and you meet just an amazing people,' said Jolie. 'Given just a little chance, and given a little help, this is going to be a great country.' She added, 'We love this country and we plan to be back over and over again.' Naturally, the media profile of their joint visit exceeded any similar missions Jolie had previously undertaken on her own.

It's worth reflecting at this point on the extent of Jolie's humanitarian work, which continues to grow admirably. At the time of writing she has visited needy people in more than twenty countries, making many of these visits before 2006 to people in places as far apart as Arizona, Sierra Leone, Tanzania, Sri Lanka and Russia. These were serious missions in which she doesn't demand celebrity comforts, but instead offers plentiful emotional comfort and hope to the unfortunate people she visits. 'We cannot close ourselves off to information and ignore the fact that millions of people are out there suffering,' she has said, explaining the essence of her involvement. She was keen to add that in her work she felt she was the same as any other type of person, famous or not. 'I honestly want to help,' she stated. 'I don't believe I feel differently from other people. I think we all want justice and equality, a chance for a life with meaning. All of us would like to believe that if we were in a bad situation someone would help us.' What a change this was from the woman who had been so notorious in her early life. Her roving ambassadorial role began to radically reposition her in the public's imagination, and her celebrity stock improved with every journey, whether that was her intention or not.

The media lapped up the couple's trips, and so Jolie and Pitt found that the Brangelina brand was something that could be used to bring attention to important causes. Not that such serious stories were ever likely to distract the public from the gossip pages, which the couple also regularly appeared in. In January 2006 rumours about their supposedly impending marriage spread like wildfire. After Pitt dined with Guy Ritchie at the exclusive Mayfair restaurant Locanda Locatelli, the *Sunday Mirror* claimed that 'all talk was about the forthcoming nuptials'. Pitt had, according to a 'source', asked Ritchie to be best man at the ceremony. 'Guy was absolutely thrilled,' the source told the newspaper. 'He thinks it's a real honour.' By now the media were so obsessed with the idea that Pitt would marry Jolie that it began piecing together its own fantasy line-up for the big day.

Celebrity chef Jamie Oliver was, according to reports, going to be doing the catering. It's true that Oliver is friends with the couple and he had said in March, 'Brad is the happiest I've seen him.' However, he had not been hired for a wedding because no wedding was going to happen. Try telling that to the world's press, though. They wanted the world's most famous couple to marry and continued to speculate over what would be a fantasy story for the media.

Later the same month the plot thickened when the *Daily Record* claimed the date had even been set for the still unconfirmed wedding. The article suggested that Pitt had phoned his ex-wife Aniston to warn her that an official announcement was pending. 'He said he was planning to get married very soon,' claimed yet another 'source'. The lack of any official word on a wedding proved to be no problem in the eyes of media editors, who knew that any story about the couple would increase their circulation, listening or viewing figures. The next theory was that the couple were to wed on Valentine's Day in Malibu, the same area where Pitt had wed Aniston. One publication went even further by claiming the couple had in fact already married. The *Daily Star* ran the sensational front page story, saying that Pitt and Jolie had exchanged vows in a secret Buddhist ceremony. 'Brad and Angelina wanted to make a commitment to each other as soon as possible and arranged a private wedding to seal their love. They exchanged vows in a Buddhist ceremony – which isn't legally binding – but in Brad and Angelina's eyes they're married.' Alongside the report was a photograph of the couple in wedding outfits, which might have leant the story some credibility in the eyes of casual browsers. However, the photograph turned out to be a still taken from *Mr. & Mrs Smith*, and the stars' representatives quickly denied the report, deriding the desperate measures the newspaper had taken to produce a wedding story for its front page.

Unabashed, the media simply found another angle as Pitt-Jolie wedding fever continued. This time the couple were said to be on the brink of marrying at the Italian villa of actor and friend George Clooney. The villa is in the town of Laglio on Lake Como, and the local residents were about to have first-hand experience of the whirlwind that surrounds Brangelina wherever they travel. Italian newspapers claimed the couple would swoop into the town on the weekend of 18 March 2006 and tie the knot, and the local police were immediately put on alert in expectation of the media interest the event would attract. The mayor, Simona Saladini, said she had been put on standby for a major event to take place in the town on the Saturday. 'I have been mayor since 2003 and they would be the most famous couple to be married here,' she said in an admirable understatement as media and fans from around the planet descended on the town. A military boat patrolled the waters near Clooney's villa, and still the lack of confirmation from the representatives of Pitt, Jolie and Clooney did nothing to deter the press or public interest. As the entire fuss turned into something of a circus, a Clooney lookalike arrived and the media – starved of an actual story to cover – gleefully interviewed and photographed him. They also took snaps of two men dressed up as Pitt and Jolie, who performed a joke wedding for the crowd. It was a moment of fun and proved a welcome distraction for reporters, who were beginning to suspect that the all-male mock wedding was the only one they were likely to be photographing that day.

Alberto Repossi, who designed the engagement ring Dodi Fayed was said to have bought for Diana, Princess of Wales, was supposed to have been commissioned to produce the wedding rings for the occasion. The media had their location and details of the jewellery, all they needed now was the couple and the sound of wedding bells. The truth was that the real Clooney's villa was undergoing renovations at the time, making it entirely unsuitable for hosting a wedding. The media might have been disappointed when they realized that Pitt and Jolie weren't in town, but the local businesses were loving it. Pietro Sacchi, owner of Harry's Bar, told the BBC, 'I doubled the number of clients this week.' In the end the media gave up, realizing that no wedding was about to take place. The same conclusion was drawn by reporters who had simultaneously surrounded a hotel in Paris where Jolie was rumoured to be staying ahead of the supposed nuptials. The media then simply changed the story from 'Pitt and Jolie are getting married' to 'Pitt and Jolie are not getting married'. Even a non-story, it seemed, was good enough to fill countless column inches and hours of airtime when it came to the subject of Brangelina. Pitt's publicist, Cindy Guagenti, attempted to bring some perspective to the situation. 'They are not getting married,' she told the press. Mindful that when it came to Brangelina even a non-story was considered a story she added, 'I don't want a story about they're not getting married. I think you guys should just drop the whole thing.' As well as covering the wedding that never was, one publication claimed that Pitt was due to buy a property next to Clooney's Italian villa as the speculation built feverishly.

By this stage, one could have picked a European country at random on a map, stuck a pin in it and the chances were that the couple had been rumoured to be getting married there at some point. Having supposedly been planning weddings in France and Italy, the next country on the phantom wedding list was Ireland. According to the *News of the World*, Pitt and

Jolie had arranged a secret ceremony in a modest venue just outside Dublin. A few weeks later, no such marriage had taken place, but anyone who expected this inconvenient truth to take the wind out of the media's sails would be proven wrong. Just two weeks later the *Herald Sun* newspaper announced that, far from planning a wedding, the couple were already married. 'Brad and Angelina have their own secret and the rings are part of it,' said the source. 'In her mind, they are married.' Having failed to marry in the European cities the press had earmarked for them, the story simply moved continents. When George Clooney arrived in Namibia in April, publications began to speculate over whether he was there to witness a Brangelina marriage, which would take the form of a traditional 'Himba' ceremony. Once again, there was no more substance to these reports beyond the fact that Clooney and Pitt are friends. Soon it was accepted that the couple's nuptials were not imminent and new unsubstantiated stories circulated that Pitt had proposed but Jolie had declined. These were duly denied.

Meanwhile Pitt and his girlfriend were finding it increasingly hard to laugh off the relentless stories – true and otherwise – being written about them. Both had been famous in their own right for years, having reached the top of their profession individually. Consequently they had become accustomed to the raft of inaccurate stories that are routinely written about anyone in the public eye. They thought they had become as famous as it was possible to be, but as a couple they discovered there were yet higher levels to which they could ascend, and as with all fame, this new stratosphere had positive and negative points. This was reflected in the couple's presence in a number of polls and surveys conducted during 2006, most of which were admiring and celebratory. The most significant came in the ACNielsen consumer survey of forty-two markets across the globe. Pitt was voted as the best male celebrity endorser for a range of product types, while Jolie came high in the female survey, beaten only by a tiny margin by Nicole Kidman. Despite narrowly missing first place, Jolie's healthy finish confirmed that the couple were a dominant force across the globe. Together they were stronger.

Jolie also took a prominent position in another highly significant poll that year. Not only was she named in the prestigious *Time* magazine's 100 most influential people of the year, she was included not in the artistic or entertainment sections, but the 'Heroes & Pioneers' category. To put this into some context, other figures included in the category for 2006 were politicians Bill Clinton and Al Gore, inspirational rock star and humanitarian Bono and survivor of the Nazi Holocaust Elie Wiesel. The accompanying text for Jolie's entry, written by Malloch Brown, Deputy Secretary General of the UN, praised her 'ability to transcend worlds' and her 'diligence and grit'. Brown concluded of Jolie's work, 'It is celebrity advocacy at its most effective, most intelligent and most sincere.' Praise indeed and from an admirable source.

The same year saw her win a less serious but still important honour when *People* magazine named her 2006's most beautiful female star. Again, her humanitarian work was honoured and considered a key part of her selection. 'She looks the most beautiful when she's in the field – natural, no makeup, nothing,' said musician Wyclef Jean, who had visited Haiti with Jolie and Pitt. 'Because you see Angelina the angel. It doesn't get any better than that.' It was a clean sweep in the *People* awards for Brangelina as Pitt finished top of the male category. 'Can you believe anyone is that good looking?' the magazine told its readers – quoting Dustin Hoffman – when unveiling Pitt as the winner. He was certainly worthy of the title as his boyish good looks had developed into a handsome and mature look now that he'd reached his forties.

Unable to conjure up a real wedding for the stunning couple, Madame Tussauds in Las Vegas planned a fake one by commissioning a 'wax wedding' for Brad and Angelina in November. A wax George Clooney would be present as Brad's best man, and the waxwork guest list was to include Elvis, Frank Sinatra,

Luciano Pavarotti, Liberace and John Wayne. Only months earlier New York's Madame Tussauds had featured the couple in a Namibian scene. In the end, the Vegas wax wedding didn't happen after Pitt's representative complained to the museum. 'I personally found it a little odd that they were re-creating a wedding that never really happened,' Ms Guagenti told the Associated Press. 'As Brad's representative, I found it disturbing.' The museum confirmed that it had called off the mock ceremony, as it was keen to maintain 'excellent relationships with the celebrity community'. It was not the first or last time the couple would have their private lives portrayed in wax, though, and they did not react so badly when the depictions were based on factual events.

What a year it had been. In December 2005 wedding rumours had started with the report of a New Year's Eve ceremony. Twelve months on, in December 2006, new wedding theories still abounded. The *Sun* newspaper proudly predicted that the wedding would take place before Christmas, and once more marriage fever swept the press. The location this time would be a village near Johannesburg, it was claimed. The star-studded guest list was to include Oprah Winfrey – who had opened a school in the area – and pop legend Madonna. The ceremony would take place to a soundtrack of tribal music apparently, and a 'pal' of the couple was quoted as saying, 'They are treating their marriage like a spiritual affirmation.' Yet again the wedding did not happen to any soundtrack, tribal or otherwise. As for the couple, they continued to quietly – and for the most part calmly – deny that marriage was imminent. The closest they came to predicting such a turn of events was when Pitt told *Esquire* magazine, 'Angie and I will consider tying the knot when everyone else in the country who wants to be married is legally able.' He later faced controversy and condemnation for his supportive nod to the campaign for civil partnerships for same-sex partners, but he stood by it regardless. Brangelina, as we shall see, was becoming an increasingly politicized force, and it was typical that they should turn the regular irritant of gossiping whispers about their lives into something positive, helping causes they believed in.

The media had gone into overdrive when covering this romance, and its prominence exceeded that given to any other famous couple at the time, including David and Victoria Beckham. It was truly astonishing, even comfortably exceeding the levels of fascination attached to recent 'supercouples' such as 'Bennifer' and 'Tom-Kat'. This was in part due to the fact that both partners in the relationship were equally famous and successful, but it was also because the public remained fascinated by the fact that Pitt had left a seemingly happy marriage with a popular woman and ended up with one of the most racy and unpredictable figures in Hollywood. Not all observers had given the relationship much of a chance at the start, but the couple appeared to be truly happy – and powerful, too. As *Entertainment Weekly* put it, 'Great role selection, a devotion to do-gooding, and a beautiful family: Angelina Jolie and Brad Pitt could teach a master class on movie stardom.'

Co-branding was becoming a more and more popular tool in the market place. In 2006 Nokia and Aston Martin combined to produce a co-branded vehicle, then sportswear giants Nike joined forces with Apple to create a running-themed iPod tool. If product brands were stronger together, it made sense that human brands would be too – even if separately they were very different to one another. Indeed, with Pitt's wholesome-but-handsome pre-Jolie image contrasting keenly with her pre-Pitt image as a lustful, erratic star who sparked rumours of incest at the drop of a kiss, combined they were a fascinating prospect. But was Jolie holding the reins of the relationship and dragging a cuckolded Pitt along with her? Or had Pitt tamed a wild beast, turning the self-harming, drug-taking Jolie into a responsible family figure?

Ultimately, we return to the couple who took the celebrity romance stakes to a new level, Richard Burton and Elizabeth Taylor. 'Brad and Angelina are today's equivalent of Richard Burton and Liz Taylor – sexy jetsetters collecting children and charities instead of jewels,' *Washington Post* columnist Amy Argetsinger told the *Irish Independent*. 'We think we know them because of their on-screen personas, though of course we don't, and that fascination with what lies behind the surface leads to the appetite for more stories about them.' That appetite has not diminished as the public's hunger for gossip on what is going on beneath the surface proves almost impossible for the media to satisfy. There was, in effect, no sign of the public saying, 'We're full.'

Instead the world was more than ready for the next course to be served up, and it wasn't just rumours of a wedding that were on the menu during 2006. The main course was the dramatic entrance, midway through the year, of the couple's first biological child.

7. The Couple Start a Family

The arrival of famous people's offspring is always greeted with huge excitement by the press and public. Indeed, just a month before Jolie gave birth to her first child, there was a media frenzy over the birth of Tom Cruise and Katie Holmes' first child, Suri. The arrival of twins to actress Julia Roberts in 2004 had also been a media extravaganza, drawing a huge global audience, and the same could be said of numerous other celebrity births, including those of the Beckhams' sons. For the public this is one of the few parts of the celebrities' lives that we can relate to and which mirror our own experiences. All of these arrivals were entirely upstaged by the birth of Pitt and Jolie's first biological child, an event that would generate literally thousands of news stories in a matter of months, prompting leading US magazine *Forbes* to name the child 'Hollywood's most influential infant'.

While Jolie was filming *The Good Shepherd* in the Dominican Republic, whispers that she might be expecting a child began to circulate. One of the first people she told was a charity worker in the Dominican Republic. 'Yes, I am pregnant,' Jolie told her on 10

January. Some forty-eight hours later Pitt's spokesperson officially confirmed the news: 'I can confirm they are expecting,' said Cindy Guagenti. Jolie had been wearing loose-fitting clothes for a while, prompting suspicions that she was pregnant. Once the news was made official she posed alongside Pitt for photographs on a trip to Haiti – now wearing a tighter outfit of T-shirt and jeans, where her bump was obvious. The photographs had been arranged in a deal with *People* magazine, for which the couple charged $500,000, all of which was generously donated to a Haitian charity. The fee seemed huge for a simple set of photos, but it wasn't surprising given that the world had been waiting for official confirmation of the couple's love for one another for quite some time – they may not have had a wedding, but they were having a baby. The photographs showed a devoted couple looking lovingly at one another, with their first child on the way. Their tranquil happiness was shaken, however, when Jolie collapsed during filming. She was, aside from her bump, very thin at this point, so there was naturally an enormous level of concern about her and she was rushed to hospital. 'She looks really frail and she's pale and gaunt,' a source told *Star* magazine. 'I heard her doctor has put her on a high-risk pregnancy alert and Brad has been trying to persuade her to go on a bed rest. But she won't hear any of it.' Jolie was soon back on set, but everyone was keeping a close eye on her.

As we saw in the previous chapter, Pitt was rumoured to have phoned Aniston to warn her about an impending wedding announcement. It was also suggested that he had telephoned his ex-wife to inform her about the pregnancy and that Jolie had also spoken to Aniston on the phone. However, Aniston's publicist insisted that no such telephone calls had occurred. 'All the reports about phone calls between Jennifer and Brad Pitt and Jennifer and Angelina Jolie are all made-up lies,' said the publicist unequivocally. Instead, Aniston had learned of the news via the media, along with the rest of the world. Friends of hers had worried since the split what her reaction would be if Pitt and Jolie went on to have a child together. When Aniston was asked how she felt about the news during an interview with *Vanity Fair* magazine, the journalist was given a first-hand glimpse of the hurt she felt. 'She looks as if I've stabbed her in the heart,' wrote the journalist in the subsequent article. 'Her eyes well up and spill over.' Aniston admitted that she had long expected a 'nauseous feeling' to come over her if such news broke, but happily she said it was not as severe as she'd feared. Disciples of astrology would argue that Aquarian Aniston would be naturally equipped to detach herself from her emotions.

Jolie's father Voight was in the same boat as Aniston, learning about his daughter's pregnancy via news reports, but he was excited at the news that he was to become a grandfather and hoped he might be able to rebuild his relationship with his daughter, who by this time hadn't spoken to him for five years. 'Now she's announced she is pregnant with Brad Pitt's child, I'd love to be included in this exciting moment,' Voight said. He added that he was 'very happy' for the pair. Only a month earlier he had said of his daughter's new man, 'I like the look of Brad. I've got a good feeling about him.'

With a child on the way, Pitt's friends rallied round him, publicly explaining how happy he was since meeting Jolie. 'He's a totally different man than he was when he was with Jennifer,' James Cruse, who has known Pitt for many years, revealed. George Clooney, who was friends with both Pitt and Aniston, explained that though their split 'really saddened' him, he was impressed with Jolie, having met her, and concluded, 'I'm happy if Brad is happy. I see them together and they look very content.' Pitt was receiving the seal of approval from many people in his life, though he had to wait a while before his parents bestowed their blessing. Both his mother and father were close to and fond of Aniston, and they were disappointed and upset when they learned that he'd left her. However, on meeting the new lady in his son's life, Pitt's father Bill told him, 'You've made the right choice, son.' While his grandmother added, 'He seems really happy.'

Both he and Jolie were indeed blissfully happy, particularly in the light of her pregnancy. Jolie admitted
late into her pregnancy that she was in 'a state of
denial' about her impending labour. After all, she had
previously maintained that herself and Pitt would
only ever adopt children. 'I was quite at peace with
that,' she said, 'and then things felt different.' They
felt different because Pitt was encouraging her to consider the biological route, as she revealed in 2010.
'When I met him . . . I didn't want to get pregnant. I
always wanted to adopt, but I never had the desire of
experiencing biological motherhood. He taught me to
be more patient and to enjoy everything that exists in
the world,' she said. She insisted that in the future the
couple would go down the adoption route again. 'We
love children, you know? So I think there's no real
plan about stopping.' The ongoing marriage rumours
were proving relentless and invasive enough, but with
the birth of their first child imminent, the world was
about to see just how powerful the couple had become
in the wake of the media circus that surrounded them.

In the latter stages of her pregnancy Jolie gave a
television interview in which she described how life
as an expectant mother was affecting her. She said
she had been 'very fortunate' overall during her
pregnancy, and had managed to avoid morning sick-
ness. However, her emotions had become turbulent,
she admitted. 'I get hysterical now,' she said. 'Like,

hysterical to the point of crying and falling off the bed . . . Like, I'll try to read, and then I'll start laughing. It'll last for, like, twenty minutes. And then, you know, I'll sit back down and focus again. He's reading and I'm reading, and we're sitting there really serious . . . and then I'll just go. Like, it'll go on for . . . for hours.' She then added, with a laugh, 'It's really horrible.' Jolie seemed on good form physically and emotionally, smiling broadly as she said, 'I have a lot to be happy about.' She also claimed that she didn't understand why there was such public interest in her relationship with Pitt, saying she found it 'kind of funny'. For someone so deft at handling that interest, her professed confusion seems a little incongruous, especially considering the way she handled the hype surrounding her forthcoming birth.

Most Hollywood stars would choose the most luxurious and modern Western hospital in which to give birth to their first child. However, as we have seen, Angelina Jolie is not like most Hollywood stars. She is a law unto herself who loves to confound expectations and test the boundaries in her life, so it shouldn't have surprised anyone that she chose a developing world country for the birth. The nation in question was Namibia in the southwest of Africa and a regular destination for Jolie. For her it was a location that made sense on a number of levels. It brought attention to the poverty and illness that afflicted so many people in Namibia, and it also was advantageous for her public image, providing another example of her famous unpredictability. Since becoming a mother she had worked to temper this image, particularly since taking up with Pitt, but she was clearly not ready to be seen as entirely conventional either. Given the anodyne and tame personalities that increasingly dominate the entertainment industry today, Jolie is a breath of fresh air in an increasingly bland arena.

There were other things to recommend her choice of birthplace – a location Pitt was allegedly opposed to until the ever-persuasive Jolie talked him round. The mansion Pitt owned in Malibu, but which the couple had yet to live in together, needed renovations and a prolonged stay overseas would mean work could continue without disrupting their lives. However, there was another reason for choosing Namibia, and sceptics believe that this was the biggest pull. Giving birth in an African hospital gave the couple a better chance of stopping the paparazzi snapping them and their new child. The determination of the press to acquire images of 'famous' babies was without restraint, and journalists weren't averse to sneaking into hospitals, as one photographer chillingly proved when he dressed up as a doctor in order to photograph Marianne Faithful, who was recovering from an overdose. Avoiding the media entirely was not an option for the couple, but they were determined to manage the story as best they could. Quite how well they would do that was underlined by the sensational revelation that the Namibian authorities would grant visas only to foreign journalists and photographers who had written permission from Pitt and Jolie to cover the birth. The audacity of even attempting such a move was breathtaking, and the fact that the couple managed to pull it off was even more amazing.

Two months ahead of the birth, Pitt and Jolie left America, stopping in Paris along the way. They were in the French capital to visit her mother Marcheline, who had been diagnosed with cancer several years earlier. Marcheline continued to struggle with her health, but dramatic reports that she was on the brink of death and had begged her daughter to give birth in France were hotly denied. It was reported that Jolie's obsession that the couple should not be seen as taking a luxurious approach to the trip began there as they stayed in a rather basic downtown tower-block apartment. After spending time with Marcheline, they moved on to Namibia, where they had booked all seven rooms and five suites at the Burning Shore seaside resort. It would become their home for the following five months, bringing the accommodation bill alone to nearly £200,000. They felt it was a price worth paying for the tighter security. 'It's very plain – it's not an upmarket establishment,' one local told the media. 'But it's situated right at the beach and you can be private.' While they waited for the baby to arrive, Pitt took the lead in looking after their two adopted children, taking them one day to the Harnas wildlife centre, where Maddox and Zahara frolicked happily with local kids while Pitt looked on proudly. This at least gave the media something concrete to write about. The conjecture at the time included a report that Pitt had bought Jolie a 'fidelity necklace' and that she was planning a water birth. Both stories were denied.

Back at the Burning Shore, the government – excited about having the world's most discussed lovers in town – leapt into action to ensure their security needs were catered for. The authorities' efforts took on an air of almost military precision as huge green barriers were erected to shield the family from the media, rogue photographers were confronted and had the film ripped from their cameras. Jolie's brother Jamie was allowed through the tight security to be at his sister's side as the due date beckoned. She had always planned to give birth at the resort, but since the baby was in breech position, she had to have a Caesarean section at the Cottage Medi-Clinic Hospital in Swakopmund. Their American surgeon Jason Roth-bart had flown to Africa to perform the operation and he was one of the first to speak to an expectant world about the details of the birth of their daughter.

'Angelina underwent a scheduled Caesarean due to breech presentation,' he confirmed. 'The baby was a healthy seven pounds. Brad was with Angelina in the operating room the entire time and cut the umbilical cord of his daughter. The surgery and birth went flawlessly.' Soon after, Jolie and Pitt confirmed that their daughter would be called Shiloh Nouvel Jolie-Pitt, contradicting the rumour that they were going to call their child Africa. While the fascinated world rushed to discover the meaning of the name, the couple warmly thanked the staff of the hospital 'for all their kindness and commitment in assuring the successful birth of our daughter'. The clinic's director Peter Sander spoke of a 'very touching' birth in which everything went 'absolutely normally'. He insisted that the famous Hollywood mum neither requested, nor was granted, any special treatment whatsoever. As for Jolie herself, she was in great spirits overall – 'feeling good, but a bit sore' – and the proud mother told an enquiring friend of her first biological child, 'The baby is beautiful.' Although everything went normally, Jolie later confessed to feeling 'suddenly terrified' as she waited for the seven-pound baby to take her first breath following the birth. Once that happened it was a moment of joyful relief for her mother, and for the rest of the world, it seemed. A headline in the *Philadelphia Inquirer* screamed, 'You can exhale, people: it's a girl for Angelina Jolie and

Angelina's starring role in the 2001 film *Tomb Raider* was to firmly cement her as the ultimate modern female sex symbol. Strong, powerful, capable and incredibly sexy, Angelina was born to play the role, and it was one she relished.

In 2005 Brad and Angelina were to star in a film that would change their lives for ever – *Mr. and Mrs. Smith*. The chemistry onscreen was as intense as a forest fire, and the months spent in training and preparation for the movie would make them incredibly close. Speculation was rife that the onscreen romance between the couple had spilled over into their private lives, but this was vehemently denied by the two actors themselves.

At the premiere of *Mr. and Mrs. Smith* the Hollywood superstars were already embroiled in a swirl of media allegations about their supposed romance. Brad described the rumours as no more than 'a good story'.

When Angelina and Brad finally went public about the nature of their relationship, it was impossible to deny that these two remarkable individuals made a seemingly beautiful and happy couple.

The couple's life together has rarely been out of the media spotlight.

It had always been a wish and dream of both Brad and Angelina to start a large family. Together, the couple have raised six children, three of which were adopted.

Above, Angelina visits a refugee camp on one of her many missions as a Goodwill Ambassador for the UN. *Below*, another side to this most remarkable of women: the picture-perfect, supportive wife.

Every picture tells a story, and with Brad and Angelina there have often appeared to be two sides. Whatever the future holds, theirs will remain one of the most talked-about Hollywood relationships of all time.

Brad Pitt', in a bid to capture the public excitement over the story.

In the wake of the birth, the couple were proving far more chatty than had been expected. Given the huge lengths and expense they had gone to in order to make the birth private it was feared they would have little to say, but in the event they proved almost loquacious as the joy of biological parenthood set in. 'It's the most amazing thing that has ever happened to us,' said Jolie. Pitt, who had looked forward to becoming a father so much, spoke particularly movingly. 'It was an amazing, beautiful, spiritual moment when our daughter Shiloh was born,' he said. 'Angelina was incredible and I feel very blessed. Our daughter is the most beautiful, precious thing.' Speaking of Shiloh's two siblings, Jolie said that Zahara seemed 'a little jealous', but added that Maddox 'loves [Shiloh]', considering her like 'a pet he can hold and look at'. She added that she had anticipated the possibility of sibling rivalry. 'I was kind of prepared to give them extra love and attention because something was going to be different about this one.' She would later explain that, contrary to the expectations of many, she actually felt more strongly for her adopted children than she did for her biological offspring. 'I feel so much more for Mad and Z because they are survivors, they came through so much. Shiloh seemed so privileged from the moment she was born, I have less inclination to feel for her. I met my other kids when they were six months, they came with a personality.'

So what did the names that Jolie and Pitt chose for their first natural child mean? Shiloh is a Hebrew name meaning 'his gift', but it's also sometimes taken to mean 'he who is sent', giving it a Messianic tinge that the media would draw on later in their coverage of the story. Nouvel is from the French word meaning 'new', and is significant because Jolie's mother has French-Canadian roots and her own middle name, Jolie – which became her surname after she dropped Voight – is also French. It's interesting to consider whether, consciously or otherwise, Jolie was making a small gesture here to her father, to whom she still wasn't speaking? By following or setting a family tradition, it certainly seemed like it to some observers. However, there was no reconciliation on the cards for father and daughter at this stage, or indeed for some time to come. Whatever the case, the name had the world fascinated, and everyone was keen to read any number of messages into it as editors sent their scribes scrambling for new angles on the sensational birth.

Jolie's brother Jamie was pounced on when he arrived back in America and asked for his verdict on the new arrival. He described how, when he saw his niece for the first time, he was so overwhelmed he walked back out of the room, adding that he'd never seen his sister as happy as she was in the wake of the birth. 'It's an exciting time for Brad and Angie, and we are really happy for them and the kids,' he told a regional American newspaper. Not the most surprising of quotes, but one that was snapped up and reproduced around the world, such was the hunger for any new titbit relating to the story. Jolie's estranged father added, 'I'm very, very excited for the both of them. My love is with them always.' Privately he hoped for a reunion so that he could hold his granddaughter in his arms.

Even the Namibian government seemed to want to stake a claim on the baby. Given that Shiloh had been born in the country, she qualified for Namibian citizenship as the government's Environment and Tourism Deputy Minister, Leon Jooste, explained. 'Shiloh Nouvel Jolie-Pitt will, according to Namibian law, be allowed to obtain Namibian citizenship if the parents should choose to do so,' he said.

The birth was the talk of the world's media, with commentators being asked for their personal take on the story in order to fill more broadcasting hours or column inches. Darryn Lyons, a colourful paparazzo and media personality, took the discussion to excruciating over-hyped new levels when he summed up the whirlwind of anticipation and public fascination with the birth by offering an analogy of almost chilling hysteria. 'I don't think [Pitt and Jolie] could have given the people more of an appetite to see the new creature,' Lyons said. 'It is the most anticipated baby since Jesus Christ.' It was a headline-grabbing statement that was quickly debunked. As one American journalist wrote in response to his use of the word 'creature', Jolie had not given birth to a salamander. More to the point, at the risk of splitting hairs, the birth of Jesus Christ was not particularly anticipated. Beyond Mary, Joseph, three wise men, some shepherds and a donkey, the rest of the world was mostly unaware of the event before it happened, though there can be no doubt of its significance since. Lyons' statement was intended semi-humorously, of course, and it did, in its exaggerated fashion, sum up the crazy level of interest surrounding the birth. Perhaps even Jolie might have admired Lyons' eye for a headline and the way it elevated the Brangelina brand to new levels.

A price was officially put on the birth when the couple sold the first authorized photos of Shiloh. The snaps were taken by the prestigious Getty Images agency at a private photo shoot. 'The photos were sent to our offices in New York and London, and customers were invited in to view the photos on site and make decisions about whether they wished to bid for them,' said Getty's CEO Jonathan Klein. He admitted that such was the tight security surrounding the bidding that not even he had been allowed to see the images.

'It's the first time we've done a major shoot where the only people who have seen the pictures are the photo editors and the sales people who are working with customers,' he said.

The winning bidder of the auction for North American rights was *People* magazine, who paid a reported $4 million for first rights on the images. Meanwhile, *Hello!* magazine won the international rights with their bid of $3.5 million. The couple attracted widespread comment for selling photographs of their children, but Pitt and Jolie were not the first to do so. It made sense, too. Not long before the actor Russell Crowe had been hounded for photographs of his son Charles. He and his wife ended up covering the baby boy in a white sheet as photographers circulated them. 'It's a terrible business, chasing kids,' admitted one photographer, but that's exactly what it was – a business. Photographs of Nicole Kidman's child, a pregnant Halle Berry or images of Britney Spears driving with a child in her lap are just some of the photographs that have achieved huge sums. *People* magazine was reported to have handed $500,000 to a Hurricane Katrina relief fund for the first photos of Britney Spears' firstborn, Sean Preston. However, the fee for Shiloh topped the lot, cementing her status, and that of her parents, as the planet's most pre-eminent celebrities.

The fee was not used, contrary to the initial cynicism

of some, to line the pockets of an already fabulously wealthy couple. Instead, they donated it to an undisclosed charity, though the nature of that charity was perhaps hinted at in the words they used when revealing the donation. 'While we celebrate the joy of the birth of our daughter, we recognize that two million babies born every year in the developing world die on the first day of their lives,' the couple said in a joint statement. 'These children can be saved, but only if governments around the world make it priority.' The couple also announced a separate $300,000 donation for the purchase of maternity-ward medical equipment for two Namibian state hospitals. 'We want to contribute to Namibia and the people who have been so gracious to us at this time,' they said in a statement. The donation, said their philanthropic adviser Trevor Neilson, 'is a thank-you and a recognition that not all parents are as lucky, that the world needs to do more to help parents who don't have access to a safe place to have their children.' This played well in the eyes of the ever-attentive court of public opinion, although there is no evidence that this was their primary motivation, of course.

Just two months into her life, Shiloh Nouvel Jolie-Pitt's fame was immortalized in the form of a model at Madame Tussauds in New York. The model, made entirely out of silicone, was featured in an African-themed nursery with models of her parents watching over her. Janine DiGioacchino, general manager at New York's Madame Tussauds, said Shiloh was 'already an iconic figure in world popular culture'. The museum said it gave the model baby her 'Mom's signature pouty lips and delicate features'. This time Tussauds acted with the blessing of 'Brangelina' who felt they had little choice but to approach the entire issue of the birth in the way they did. It is worth noting, however, that some stars have a different approach to the public's interest in the birth of their babies. When actress Sarah Jessica Parker gave birth to her son James in 2002 she was expected to charge a large fee for the first photographs of her boy. Instead, she simply tipped off the press about what time and through which door she would exit the hospital and posed for several minutes as the snappers got all the images they wanted.

In contrast to Jolie's post-birth admission that she was extra protective of her two adopted children's feelings, Pitt said that he considered all three children to be his and encouraged other prospective parents to consider adoption. 'They're as much of my blood as any natural born, and I'm theirs,' he told *Esquire* magazine. 'That's all I can say about it. I can't live without them. So: Anyone considering [adoption], that's my vote.' Asked by the magazine what his parenting style was, the man who had for so long dreamt of becoming a father described himself in laid-back terms. 'I try not to stifle them in any way,' he said. 'If it's not hurting anyone, I want them to be able to explore. Sometimes that means they're quite rambunctious. I feel it's really important to have that time to sit and talk to them,' he continues. 'I really like that last minute before they fade off. And always give them a heads-up before you jerk them out of something. You need to tell them, like, "You have three more minutes."'

The now five-strong family left Namibia in June after a two-month stay. 'We are very proud that our daughter was born here, and we leave with fond memories and definitely hungry to return,' Pitt said as they left. It had been quite a stay. The Namibian people and authorities had mixed feelings as they left. In part they were relieved that the circus had packed up and gone home, but they were also sad that Namibia's place at the epicentre of the biggest celebrity story of the modern era was over. The couple were immensely grateful for the way the people of Namibia had treated them during their stay. 'They've been so gracious to us and made our stay here very special, and because of that . . . we've had an incredible time with our family exploring the country, and a truly peaceful birth of our daughter . . . we will certainly be back.' With that they returned to the more familiar surroundings of Los Angeles. Their sojurn in Africa had certainly been attention grabbing, and it was soon suggested that pop singer Britney Spears would follow suit by giving birth there, though to date that appears to be just another rumour.

As we have seen, Jolie's father Voight had hoped for a reconciliation with his daughter in the wake of Shiloh's birth and the proud grandfather was keen to meet the newborn girl. Although the couple kept their distance from him, the social circles of Los Angeles made it hard for them to avoid one another completely, and when the Jolie-Pitts rolled up at the Hollywood birthday party of *Oceans* franchise co-star Scott Caan in August they heard that Jolie's father was also present at the party. The world's most famous couple were reduced to cowering outside the party in their car for thirty excruciating minutes. Eventually, Pitt nipped into the party to offer his best wishes to Caan and shortly afterwards Voight left. Only then did Jolie make her entrance, arriving inauspiciously via the back door. It wasn't the sort of attention-grabbing entrance she was used to making, and the evening was a reminder that even the most powerful celebrities in the world are not immune to the tensions, trials and awkwardness that come with being part of a family.

As for the hapless Voight, he must have had many moments of regret for his part in the events that led to his daughter disowning him. What a strange experience it must be for a father to be estranged from his daughter, yet still be aware of her every move, thanks to the world's media. There must be many fathers with perfectly healthy relationships with their offspring who are less aware of their children's day-to-day lives than Voight is with Jolie's. Voight remained as optimistic as he could about a rapprochement, and sent expensive baby gifts to the family's home in the hope of thawing relations between them.

In November the Jolie-Pitts visited Cambodia, where they were shown around a former Khmer Rouge death camp, which has been transformed into a consciousness-raising museum about the history of genocide. Jolie also discussed environmental issues with the Cambodian authorities during their stay. They then travelled to Vietnam where, somewhat ironically, they spent American Thanksgiving weekend, which they marked not with a turkey-eating feast but with a motorbike ride round Ho Chi Minh City. Motorbikes are a popular mode of transport in the city, and the increasingly responsible-seeming Jolie managed a brush with her wilder side as she rode pillion behind her husband. Both were pictured by the Associated Press not wearing crash helmets, and though this didn't break any laws it was still commented upon; it wouldn't be the last time that road safety would be an issue for them either. Later that day they dined at a popular restaurant in a converted old temple, finishing off a trip that would have a significant legacy for the Pitt-Jolie household, though this would not become clear for some months.

In December Jolie gave a light-hearted interview to *People* magazine where she offered some interesting insights into life in their household. When asked who was the family disciplinarian, Jolie replied, 'I am. Brad can be, but if Z doesn't get the bottle from me, she'll very quickly run to Daddy.' But, asked the interviewer, which of the children had the most power in the home? 'I bet if you asked Brad, he'd say Zahara,' said Jolie of their middle child, who was just approaching her second birthday. 'Mad[dox] is very smart, but he's got a certain sense of calm,' she continued. 'Zahara is possibly the funniest person I've ever met in my life. So dramatic and creative and loud and charming,' Jolie says. 'She's definitely the biggest personality in the house.' The often tough-talking Jolie showed a more vulnerable side when she reacted emotionally to some praise she and Pitt had received about their parenting skills. 'Somebody said to us recently that they were happy kids, and we talked about how much that meant to us to hear,' she said. 'And they're good kids. God knows how we managed to do that but they're good kids.' The United Nations Brangelina brood seemed to be in good hands.

As 2006 drew to a close, Pitt and Jolie should have

been happier than ever. Although they hadn't married, their relationship seemed at its most stable and they'd had their first natural child together, adding to their two beloved adopted siblings. Pitt had adopted Maddox and Zahara, and he was the natural father of Shiloh. Jolie spoke glowingly of her man, saying, 'He's a great challenge to me. We push each other to be better.' But when Jolie was asked yet again about whether she and Pitt would marry, her words had – in retrospect at least – a troubling air. 'We are legally bound to our children, not to each other, and I think that's the most important thing,' she said. Three more children would soon swell the family's home, but even with six Jolie-Pitts running around, the proud parents found it hard to dispel the whispers that their relationship was becoming rocky. They would soon be reminded that for all the advantages and benefits of their fame, and all the power of brand Brangelina, there is a price to pay for superstardom.

8. Trouble in Paradise?

It is worth recalling at this point the glamorous life-styles that Pitt and Jolie enjoy. They are world famous and have a combined fortune that runs to an estimated several hundred million dollars. They can pick and choose which projects they take in a lucrative industry, then travel the world on private jets. Such fame and fortune comes at a cost, though. Over the coming year the media would become increasingly intrusive with its incessant coverage of their lives as the Brangelina brand became more and more profitable for the people of the press. Neither Pitt nor Jolie were strangers to such treatment, but even they would be surprised at how things developed. It was to prove a testing twelve months for them, an 'annus horribilis' one could accurately say.

For Jolie the year began with a tragedy when she was dealt the most devastating blow of her life to date. Her mother Marcheline Bertrand had bravely battled ovarian cancer for seven years, but on 27 January 2007 she finally succumbed to the illness. Jolie had been warned by doctors that the end was near for her beloved mother, and she and Pitt rushed to the

Cedars-Sinai Hospital on Beverly Boulevard in Los Angeles, arriving just hours before her mother died. Her brother Jamie was present too when Marcheline slipped away, and the siblings released a joint statement that read, 'There are no words to express what an amazing woman and mother she was. She was our best friend.' The family asked that rather than sending flowers, people donate to the Women's Cancer Research Institute at Cedars-Sinai Medical Center.

Although her mother's death was not a shock, given her condition, Jolie had remained positive until the end. Just weeks earlier she had told CNN's Larry King that her mother was 'doing good' in her fight for life. 'She's a remarkable woman. She's very, very strong and her spirit remains unbroken.' However, she was forced to say goodbye to her mother on that traumatic Saturday afternoon in January. There were reports that at the last moment of her life Marcheline made a moving and specific appeal to her daughter. She took Jolie's hand, looked into her eyes and, speaking of Pitt, told her, 'You marry that man. He's an angel sent to look after you.' She had been encouraging her daughter to tie the knot with Pitt for some months, but when that request turned out to be her dying wish it was a moving and potent moment that was said to leave Jolie 'utterly choked'.

In Marcheline's last hours, and in those immediately following her passing away, Pitt was a heroic presence for Jolie and her brother, as Jolie recalled later in the year. 'He sat with me and held my hand,' she said. 'After she passed away he spent the night asking me and my brother about our mother and getting us to tell funny stories about her. He focused on all the love and joy we were fortunate enough to have had. He was extraordinary.' A private funeral was held for Marcheline, and her mother's death left Jolie feeling as though she'd lost both her parents. Although Voight was still alive, their estrangement meant she effectively considered herself parentless. A friend told the press, 'Marcheline's death has done nothing to heal the rift between Angie and her father. She's never forgiven him for abandoning them and I believe she will take that resentment to her grave. She was dreading this moment. She felt she had already lost her father – and now her mom too.'

If Voight felt that the passing of his ex-wife might prompt a reunion with his daughter, he was to be disappointed. But was Jolie of a mind to fulfil her mother's dying wish that she marry Pitt? A friend immediately predicted that, although Jolie had always dreamt that if they did tie the knot it would be her mother who would give her away at the ceremony, the couple would soon wed. If she did so, said the friend, she would be fulfilling a long-standing wish not just of her mother, but of Pitt himself. 'Brad has never stopped trying to push her down the aisle,' said the friend. Jolie appeared to hint that her man was the keen one when she said, 'It's a touchy subject.' However, other sources suggest that the opposite is true. Pitt's grandmother, Betty Russell, insists that a lingering sense of guilt from his failed first marriage to Aniston has made the superstar reluctant to take the plunge again. 'Brad promised his last wife on their wedding day that they'd be together forever and they didn't make it,' she said. 'He is a sensitive soul who just wants to make sure he can keep his promise this time.' Reports suggested that not only were the couple at odds over the subject of marriage, but also over the question of further adoptions. Pitt was said initially to be against the idea of adopting another child in the wake of Shiloh's birth, but Jolie was keen to do so. 'Next we'll adopt,' she said confidently. 'We don't know what country. It's gonna be a balance of what's right for Maddox and Z right now. It's, you know, another boy, another girl, which country, which race would fit in best with the kids.' Jolie had her heart set on building a huge family with as many as thirteen children, but although she found childbirth easier than expected she was clear that many of her future children would come via adoption. 'I sure as hell ain't squeezing all those out,' she said – not an unreasonable stance to take given the numbers involved. After Shiloh's birth she'd been happy but very tired. 'I don't know how I am going to get myself together again,' she had complained, expressing a feeling that many mothers will readily relate to.

According to press reports in January, the adoption issue was also the subject of controversy between Jolie and the singer Madonna. According to the *Mail on Sunday* Jolie had advised Madonna to adopt from Ethiopia, as she had with Zahara. However, the singer ended up choosing a child from Malawi – a decision that infuriated Jolie, who told a French magazine, 'Madonna knew the situation in Malawi, where he was born. It's a country where there is no legal framework for adoption.' Madonna was angry with Jolie for criticizing her and took a swipe at her plans to build orphanages. 'I'm not interested in going there like an idiot and going, "OK, I'm going to build ten orphanages and I'll see you guys later,"' she stormed. An unnamed friend of Madonna's attacked Jolie for 'seeming to think she has got a monopoly on being the good Samaritan'. It was a touch unsettling to watch these two wealthy, famous women squabbling over their compassionate work, and the spat only fuelled scepticism over the motivation behind celebrities' humanitarian work. It also underlined the dilemma stars face when working for good causes. If they are public about their work they're accused of vanity, but if they don't reveal their work they deprive their adopted causes of much-needed publicity. As we shall see, Jolie's compassionate efforts would be doubted by another celebrity in 2008, only this time the attack was on the record and very fierce.

According to a source quoted in *Grazia* magazine, Jolie's humanitarian work was proving a source of concern for those closest to her, including Pitt and her brother. 'Brad and James adore Angelina for her endless quest to make the world a better place, but they worry about her not eating or sleeping enough,' said the source. 'Her mother Marcheline's death has put pressure on her and this may partly explain the weight loss. But everyone is worried that her way of coping is by throwing herself into her UN work and looking after her kids – with scant regard for herself.' Whatever the origin of these quotes, the story served only to portray Jolie as a selfless, responsible woman, rather than the feral creature she had once appeared to be. The Madonna controversy aside, the adoption route was an attractive one for Jolie and she was keen to add to her brood sooner rather than later, as she told the *Mirror*. 'Brad's great, and a really dedicated father,' she said. 'I'm very fortunate to have him in my life. We take turns working and we both love being with our kids – it's something we're enjoying very much. We shouldn't stretch it out over the next ten years because we'll be raising kids forever. So we've thought about it and I'm sure we won't wait forever to build our family.'

They would not wait forever. Just six weeks after

her mother's death they adopted a three-year-old Vietnamese child called Pham Quang, renaming him Pax Thien Jolie. Angelina filed adoption papers at the end of February, then visited the Tam Binh Orphanage in Ho Chi Minh city. She and Pitt had first visited the orphanage during their Thanksgiving stay in 2006, when they'd motorcycled round the city. Jolie returned in March 2007 with her son Maddox at her side while Pitt was busy filming in California. Their mission was to collect the new addition to the family, but the visit did not exactly go as planned.

Orphanage director Nguyen Van Trung explained that it was not a perfect fairytale moment as Jolie collected her son. 'He woke up at 6 a.m., just like all the children. He put on new clothes and he was very excited.' When Jolie arrived, she knelt down and gave her new son a kiss and a cuddle, but he burst into tears. In her first act of motherhood towards him, Jolie took Pax to one side and comforted him. 'She told me she understands that it's normal for a child to be scared and she seemed very good at getting along with children,' added Mr Trung. 'Later he was OK, very cheerful and happy. He even played with his new brother Maddox.' Jolie was said to have spent only twenty minutes in the orphanage collecting Pax, who was then carried to a waiting car with his face covered by an umbrella to hide him from the waiting photographers. Jolie then rushed to the car, which had darkened windows, and they drove to a nearby centre to perform the formal adoption ceremony. During the ceremony Jolie was very emotional and was said to have sobbed as the paperwork was completed, making Pax officially her son and the fourth member of her family. It had been an eventful and emotional day and it was still only 9 a.m.

Although Pitt had legally become the father of Jolie's two previously adopted children, Jolie legally adopted Pax alone. Vietnamese law does not allow unmarried couples to adopt, but does allow lone parents to, so Jolie going it alone was a way to get round the law. In time she changed the child's name to Pax Thien Jolie-Pitt by filing papers at the Los Angeles County Superior Court to symbolically make Pitt the father. In the meantime, though, having obtained a visa for her son from the American embassy in Hanoi, Jolie flew home in a private jet with Pax and Maddox at her side. Here came the first hint that she was ready to take a step back from her career to concentrate fully on motherhood. 'I will stay home with Pax and help him adjust to his new life,' she said. 'I have four children, and caring for them is the most important thing to me at the moment.' As we shall see, however, Jolie was to make a habit of announcing retirements – or semi-retirements.

The gossip about Jolie's impending retirement was never proved correct, but this didn't trouble the media. Having unsuccessfully predicted a Pitt-Jolie wedding in 2006 they continued speculating about the marriage throughout the following year. In March 2007, for instance, the *Daily Star* predicted an Easter wedding in the Dominican Republic. Pax and Maddox were lined up as pageboys for the ceremony, at which Shiloh would also be present. 'While they were in the Dominican Republic, Brad bought a huge tract of land and helped to design a fabulous house,' said a source. 'It's there they intend to become Mr and Mrs Pitt. They were first photographed there as a family and the place holds so many special memories for them.' Easter came and went without a marriage taking place, however, proving yet another media story false. It would not be the last by any means.

Happily, harrowing reports of a kidnap attempt on Pax also never came true. At the end of March, according to the *Sun*, the couple were made aware of a 'credible and meticulously planned' plot to snatch Pax and demand a huge ransom. 'They're highly skilled operatives with little regard for human life,' said a source. 'The gang ordered their LA members to devise a plan to kidnap Pax before demanding a ransom of $50 million – equal to the profit from a year of drug dealing.' A friend of the couple claimed that Jolie, who had already lost a great deal of weight in the aftermath of Shiloh's birth, was shedding more pounds and sleeping fitfully due to her fears over the threat. It was another reminder for her, and the world, of the downside of fame and fortune. She and Pitt would be forced to remain strong and vigilant as their family grew and developed.

It was at such moments of almost unimaginable vulnerability, said those close to her, that Jolie most benefitted from Pitt's presence in her life. 'Brad has changed my sister a lot,' said her brother Jamie in the wake of the kidnap threat. 'They have an extraordinary bond, it's not on the usual level. He's great with her and I've never seen a brood like that who are all so supportive of one another. Brad is so strong for her. When she feels vulnerable, he has the most incredible strength. She says she couldn't have adopted more children after Maddox without him. I've never seen any sign of tension between them, and if it keeps going the way it's going, they'll be together for life.' Jolie, speaking to *Readers' Digest* in May, also painted an image of familial harmony, and explained how they tried to ensure that each child received equal love and attention. 'We've tried to figure out a lot of private time for each of them,' Jolie told *Reader's Digest*. 'When everybody goes to bed, we give Mad time. When everybody is at school, we give Shiloh time. In between, Z and Pax each get special time. And on Sundays we have a big family sleep, when the boys get in bed with us and we watch a movie. It started with Mad, then Pax, and now Z is desperate to move into the bed.'

If these words were designed to stave off the mounting rumours that all was not well in the Jolie-Pitt household, then they failed to paper over the perceived cracks in their relationship. As they travelled to the Cannes Film Festival, where *A Mighty Heart* was to be premiered, they became aware of the growing whispers. When they sat in front of the press in Cannes, Jolie felt moved to respond to the rumours. 'We arrived here on Sunday and had a beautiful day with our kids,' she said firmly. 'We're here as a family and have been playing with the children since the moment we landed. We want to enjoy this with our family and friends.' Pitt was at her side and agreed with her remarks, attempting to close the press conference on a light note by saying, 'Yeah, whatever what's-her-name said.'

While Jolie insisted that her relationship with Pitt was happy and tranquil, she admitted to the American breakfast television show NBC *Today* that 2007 was proving a testing time for her. 'This has been a heavy year, in losing my mum and having a fourth child,' she told viewers. 'I am very aware of time and memories, and doing and enjoying life. I lost my mum, it's a natural thing for a child to lose a parent. I lost my mum too young, but it happens and I am happy she is not in pain – because I love her.'

In the meantime, Jennifer Aniston might have been gone from Pitt's day-to-day life, but she was not forgotten, by the media in particular. In June 2007 the newsstands proved that as far as the press was concerned the Pitt/Jolie/Aniston love triangle was still worth commenting on. In the same month *New!* magazine put Jolie on the front cover with the headline 'Angelina's Breakdown', and *Look* magazine put Aniston on their cover with the headline 'Jen's Shock Breakdown'. Aniston's continued closeness to Pitt's mother Jane only served to keep her in focus. Nobody, it seemed, was quite willing to give up hope that Hollywood's golden couple might get back together. Naturally, reports of both their 'breakdowns' were much exaggerated, as front cover headlines often are in such a cut-throat competitive market. The two ladies would once more find themselves side by side on the newsstands as their lives again became entwined, to the intense upset and fury of Jolie but the joy of the public, who had long dreamt of a fairytale reunion between Pitt and his former wife.

On the day after her thirty-second birthday in June, Jolie visited a Catholic orphanage in Prague, where she was filming *Wanted*, an action film based on the comic series of the same name. She identified one child in particular, claimed the *Sun*, and telephoned Pitt to suggest another adoption. 'Her maternal instincts are in overdrive and she felt a bond with the kid straight away,' claimed a source in the report. 'She called Brad and said she had found a child who would fit in perfectly with the other kids. If everything goes smoothly, Angelina will have an Eastern European son to add to her brood.' No such adoption was forthcoming and it appears that Jolie was merely visiting the orphanage out of a sense of solidarity with those who ran it. Indeed, as she told *Marie Claire* magazine, she and Pitt were finding it hard enough to juggle their parenting and professional duties as it was. They were discovering that grabbing any 'me time' at all was a tall order. 'Right now, we're not great about Mommy-and-Daddy time,' she confessed. 'Mommy and Daddy need to try to figure out more time right now. We're working on it, we're working on it'. Adopting another child at this point was not going to be part of working on it, clearly.

In a separate interview in the same month she reminded the public that she and Pitt had never had a childless time together. She already had Maddox when they got together and since then three more children had come along. 'Some people have their lives together and then they have their children,' she told *Esquire*. 'Brad and I are starting with the children and are planning to have our time together in our later years.' She also reprised her theme of the couple struggling to find time for themselves amid their hectic schedules and responsibilities. 'We hardly ever leave the house,' she explained. 'We try to schedule time when we're alone.' Naturally, when they did manage to grab some quiet time together out and about, they were invariably interrupted by journalists, photographers or autograph hunters. When you're as recognizable as Pitt and Jolie, there can never be true solitude. Theirs is a level of fame that even some of Hollywood's biggest names haven't experienced. Matt Damon is a world-famous actor, but he has watched aghast at the price they pay for their fame. 'I honestly don't know how Brad does it. He can't walk down the street anywhere, literally anywhere,' Damon told *Empire* magazine. 'They're in Prague right now because Angelina's working, and he can't walk down the street.'

The increasing pressure from the outside world must have put a strain on the couple's relationship, and at times this meant the couple had to take special measures to ensure privacy on family outings. For instance, in July they hired out an entire bowling alley in France so they and the children could play in private. Even after taking such measures they still found that details of their lives were made public. The bowling alley owner Patrick Bernard was quoted in *People* magazine as saying, 'At one point . . . because the children don't have the strength to always get the ball down the lane, it sometimes stops. Brad thought he'd go down the lane to push it along. He slipped and fell on his back. We're certainly the smallest bowling alley in France, so we're still having trouble realizing we spent Monday afternoon with the most famous couple in the world.' He hadn't shared painfully intrusive details of the couple's lives, but the fact that he spoke to the media at all shows that the couple can never be fully private whatever steps they take. Although that episode had taken place in France, Pitt began to wonder whether they should move away from Hollywood to mainland Europe, in part to lessen the brightness of the media glare, but also for reasons related to their quest for private happiness and well-being.

'I want Angelina to settle down somewhere out of the limelight,' he told a friend. 'She's lost a lot of weight recently and our plans are strictly to do with our move to Berlin. She wants to leave acting and support me with this. We also don't want our kids to go to school in Hollywood – it will be best if they can go to school in Berlin. We love the city. Berlin is so quiet and balanced, away from paparazzi.' Jolie had recently admitted during an interview that her weight was proving an issue for her, particularly since her mother's death in January. 'I've always been lean and this year I lost my mum so I've been through a lot,' she said. 'I have four kids and I finished breastfeeding. It's been hard to get my nutrition back on track.' Could Pitt's itchy feet be related to problems in their relationship?

The whispers about their relationship being in serious trouble were getting louder all the time. Their trip to France had been designed to improve their relationship, but according to *Life&Style* magazine their stay was riddled with problems. A source claimed they had a row during a meal when Pitt accused Jolie of behaving in an immature fashion. 'Brad's had enough of doing what Angie wants to do and following her around the globe.' Nonetheless, Pitt's representative denied their relationship was in trouble and accused reporters of 'writing lies'. However, from this summer onwards Pitt and Jolie began to face more or less non-stop speculation that their relationship was in trouble. When they were forced to cancel a planned holiday in the Lake Mohawk region of New Jersey because of Pitt's work commitments, Jolie was furious and reportedly pinned up a sign on their kitchen wall that said, 'Success is a beast, it puts the emphasis on the wrong thing. I prefer to look within.'

The month of August threw up two further stories that showed the extreme contrasts present in the life of a celebrity like Brad Pitt. It was revealed that in Australia, a special postage stamp featuring Jolie and Pitt was to be issued. The stamp would be the front cover image of the edition of *New Life* magazine which featured the couple and promoted record-breaking sales. As news of this honour broke, Pitt was arriving at a Los Angeles court wearing a T-shirt, jeans and a baseball cap. He was there to do jury service, proving that even one of the most famous men in the world still has to do his civic duties. Happily for Pitt, the defendant in his allotted case – a drink driving charge – pleaded guilty, so he and his fellow jury members were not required. At least the postage stamp story dispelled some of the relentless coverage of the couple's supposedly rocky relationship, even if only for a few days.

Controversy was to stalk them determinedly from now on. Later in August Jolie was said to be house-hunting alone after having a private viewing of a $2 million luxury villa in Laurel Canyon. The owner of the villa, Wolfgang Wing, said, 'It was very strange because it was just her, no bodyguard, no assistant, no nanny, no kids and no Brad. I had no idea who the potential buyer was until I saw her.' He added that Jolie was 'extremely skinny'. The image of a painfully thin woman viewing a new property alone was a powerful one that gave credence to the theory of an impending split. Some time later Jolie was interviewed by the French magazine *Public* and spoke of the inherent trust she had earned from Pitt and how her more colourful sexual ways were behind her. 'I've never hidden my bisexuality. But since I've been with Brad, there's no longer a place for that or S&M in my life.' She claimed that, contrary to the image of her as a sexually charged daredevil, she had only slept with four men – 'and I married two of them!' Was the sexual vixen Jolie in truth a more demure and tame creature?

Ironically, public statements such as these only served to feed the groundswell of belief that all was not well in her marriage. The maxim that actions speak louder than words would be tested as the couple began to try for another biological child. 'Yes, we're ready for another,' Pitt announced. Aside from getting married – a course of action they were still regularly rumoured to be about to undertake – this was perhaps the only action they could take to challenge the belief that there was trouble in paradise. Pitt was said to be particularly hopeful that their next child would be a boy, though he denied the suggestion that they were on the brink of adopting an Ethiopian boy to add to their brood. The next child, he hoped, would be a natural one. He would get his way – and twofold.

Far from finding pregnancy a problem in the bedroom department, it seemed that both Pitt and Jolie found it a turn-on. 'I loved being pregnant and fortunately I was with a man who found it sexy, too,' Jolie confessed in *Marie Claire* magazine. 'In the weeks before the birth we'd have dinner in the dunes by candlelight. We would have a tent out by the ocean.' She also found Pitt's widely praised parenting skills a turn-on. 'I mean, there's nothing sexier than a man who is a great father.' She smiled. Pitt will have been warmed by these words because, at the age of forty-three, he was feeling less attractive all the time. Speaking of life in his forties he had said, 'One thing sucks, your face kind of goes.' A few months later he predicted that in future film roles one sort of action would be out of the question for him. 'I can't see any more nude scenes,' he sighed. As for Jolie, she said that she continued to enjoy sexual scenes in her films. It was good to hear that she hadn't completely calmed down.

According to *Life&Style* magazine, the trust Jolie claimed Pitt had in her was not reciprocated. Jolie was said to be a suspicious figure around the home, going through his pockets and asking to see the emails he sent to his ex-wife Aniston. 'She turns everything on its head and tries to make Brad the villain,' said an insider, according to the report, though a later pronouncement refuted the claims. Although they were no strangers to press intrusion the couple now faced an almost unimaginable level of interest in their relationship, and the fact that so much of it was ghoulish and longing for scandal made it even harder to cope with. Other famous people, who were used to a certain amount of media interest themselves, looked on in horror, Jolie's ex-husband Billy Bob Thornton among them. He had remained friends with Jolie and was on good terms with Pitt. 'I do feel sorry for Angie and Brad,' he commented as the rumour mill continued to churn out speculation. 'The only time you hear about me is when I've got a movie coming out and I like it like that. They have to cope with it all the time.'

In response to their growing level of fame the couple didn't always act in ways that portrayed them in a positive light, as the following episodes prove. When Jolie was promoting her film *A Mighty Heart* in the summer of 2007, the usual queue of reporters applied for an interview with the star. Jolie had, of course, been through this process numerous times, but this was the first time reporters had been asked to sign a contract before being allowed face to face with her. Some of the contract's stipulations were that the interviewer 'will not ask Ms Jolie any questions about her personal relationships', while further down the contract was an even more restrictive clause, asking for a promise that the interview would not be used 'in a manner that is disparaging, demeaning or derogatory to Ms Jolie'. The press were horrified – not least because *A Mighty Heart* conveys a powerful message about press freedom. Jolie's behaviour seemed distastefully ironic under the circumstances, and it wasn't long before journalists and publications threatened to boycott covering the film. The contract was soon withdrawn, followed by claims that there had been a mistake involving an 'overzealous lawyer'.

Some parents who sent their children to the Lycée

Français de New York felt that the school authorities were being overzealous when they sent letters home to parents asking them to stop approaching Pitt and Jolie as they dropped Maddox off in the morning and collected him in the afternoon. 'Regretfully, I have seen some parents taking pictures, asking for autographs, talking to the media and even shouting at Ms Jolie and Mr Pitt for recognition,' read the letter. 'Therefore, in the best interests of the school and safety of your child(ren) I must ask for everyone to please respect the family's privacy and discontinue these practices.' In their different ways, both the contract and school incident showed the no-win situation the couple found themselves in. The invasiveness they faced might have shocked fellow celebrities, but when they took steps to protect their privacy it only made them look like divas or a couple with something to hide. The public may be increasingly preoccupied with celebrities, but we are not always as fair as we are fascinated.

In late October 2007 Pitt admitted what many had suspected for some time: that he was keen to marry Jolie. 'I still want to kiss the bride, wear the ring, wear my suit and wake up in the morning and say, "Good morning wife",' he admitted. For a man who had grown up in a close loving family this desire seems natural and intense. He also spoke again of his wish to settle in Europe. There, he felt, they would be afforded more privacy, and he also felt that their humanitarian work would be more respected in Europe than it was in America. Their trips to Asia and Africa would also be less of a slog from a European starting point. Mostly, though, it was the increased privacy he craved, because he had noted the effect their fame was having on the children, who he said were terrified of the paparazzi.

'It's out of hand and crosses all lines of decency; the kids didn't ask for this and it's frightening,' he said. 'They get right in the kids' faces with video cameras and yell their names. This is their idea of the world they live in. My two-year-old [Zahara] hates it. Hates the cameras.' Pitt's concern for his children was moving, not least because it came at the same time as Jolie fell pregnant again. There was speculation that Jolie might be pregnant again at the end of October, when she pulled out of doing a lecture about the future of mankind, which she was due to deliver at the Pio Manzù Centre in Rimini, Italy, but an official announcement of her pregnancy would have to wait.

Meanwhile the third member of the love triangle re-emerged into the picture. Jennifer Aniston had dated other famous men since splitting with Pitt, most notably comedy actor Vince Vaughn and singer John Mayer. For the public, though, she had never left the picture as far as Pitt was concerned, and the drip-drip of stories suggesting the pair might still be in contact continued to build in volume. In November, *W* magazine featured two covers, one of Jolie and one of Aniston – two years on from *Mr. & Mrs. Smith* and the media was as keen as ever to prompt a cat fight between Pitt's former and current lovers. During a press conference that month to promote *Beowulf*, Jolie was asked for her opinion on the *W* covers. 'Why would I comment on that?' she snapped. 'That matters because . . . ?' The question had clearly touched a nerve, and the days when Jolie had said she would be willing to meet up with Aniston seemed an age away.

Aniston also still regularly met up with Pitt's mother Jane, and this continued to be an issue for Jolie and Pitt, according to Aniston's friend Tiffany Law. Law told *Star* magazine, 'Jen sees no reason to stop [contact with Jane]. They speak on the phone at least once a month and exchange cards and emails.' Within weeks of this it was reported that Aniston still called Jane 'mum', which cannot have pleased Jolie.

She would soon have a more important issue to worry about. In the early hours of 27 November the couple were awakened by the sound of gunfire outside their Los Feliz home. A security truck parked outside their home had been shot at by a passing car and a Range Rover belonging to a neighbour had also been struck. Although it transpired that the shooting wasn't targeted at them in any way, the incident was still upsetting for the couple. They had been made aware of threats in the past, including alleged kidnap plans against their children, but in the wake of this incident they reviewed and tightened their security measures. 'You can tell their security guys are on high alert now,' said a neighbour. Two months later a freelance journalist hanging round outside their home was arrested, and soon after that *Life&Style* magazine claimed that an intruder had left a threatening note about Shiloh on the family's doorstep. Pitt furiously rejected the story, raging, 'This is absolutely not true and it's reckless and dangerous to put these ideas out into the world.' As for Jolie, she had a major scare one day when she awoke and couldn't find Shiloh. 'I'd taken a nap and Shiloh was asleep in her cradle and when I woke up she was gone,' she remembered. 'I was freaking out. And nothing had happened. Brad had taken her and the rest of the kids to the park. I love Brad, and if anything happened to him it would wreck me, but if anything happened to my kids . . . it's something I can't even think about. It's so upsetting.'

It had been a testing year for the family in many ways, but they hoped the festive season would bring some cheer and respite. Jolie, who like Aniston admitted to being a poor cook, planned to prepare the family's Christmas meal, but admitted, 'I've never really cooked before. But this year I'm going to try to cook a turkey with the kids. In case it doesn't work out, we'll have a pizza waiting.' Jolie had shed so much weight during the year that some might argue she could do with eating a traditional Christmas meal *and* a pizza in a bid to get back to a healthier weight. Jolie was insistent, though, that the pounds she'd lost were not the result of trying to be skinny out of vanity, but rather a reaction to her grief over the loss of her beloved mother. 'The thing that's disturbing is that instead of people saying, "This looks like a person that's actually dealing with something, probably from emotions," they say, "Does she fit into skinny jeans and look thin?"' she said. 'I want people to understand who I am as a person is not somebody that's trying to look thin, but just trying to work through a very difficult year.'

One of their biggest priorities for the year ahead was presenting a harmonious front to the public in face of growing suspicions that their relationship was embattled. Could Pitt and Jolie silence the doubters? Or would the scepticism and intrusion escalate to even more intense and painful levels?

9. A United Front

Although naming a date for a wedding would have been one way for Jolie and Pitt to silence the whispers that their relationship was rocky, it was not the only option open to them. Nor was it necessarily the best route. After all, the cynical public might just as easily think the wedding was a sham to throw them off the scent. If Jolie was to fall pregnant again, though, it would not only suggest that they had long-term plans together, but that physically their relationship remained passionate. Meanwhile the media circus that would inevitably surround the story would cement their brand and could be used to financially benefit the couple's many charitable causes. Jolie's second pregnancy was certainly convenient for them, even though they claim it was unplanned. Whatever the case, Jolie had a birth to look forward to and the media had another nine-month obsession ahead. First, though, the press had to confirm the news, which was officially kept under wraps for a while.

After the cancellation of Jolie's Italian talk in 2007 suspicion had grown that Jolie was expecting another baby. At the start of 2008 these rumours increased, particularly after she drank water all evening at the Critics' Choice Awards in January and then wore a maternity-style dress to the Screen Actors Guild Awards. In the same month the story became even more exciting when it was suggested that she was expecting twins. 'Brad and Angelina are absolutely ecstatic,' a source told *Star* magazine. This time the 'source' was spot on, though the story wasn't officially confirmed for some time as the stars' representatives refused to comment one way or another.

Meanwhile, Aniston continued to take a leading role in Brangelina's press coverage. In February, Pitt and Jolie failed to appear at a pre-Oscars party they were co-hosting. The press claimed they had decided not to attend in order to avoid bumping into Aniston, for fear of upsetting her with their presence. 'Angie is an incredibly strong but also incredibly sensitive woman, and she would always be careful when another woman's feelings are concerned,' Jolie's brother Jamie Haven said. Instead they showed up at the Film Independent Spirit Awards and everyone there noticed that Jolie had what appeared to be a 'baby bump'. Pitt's pal George Clooney was asked whether he knew the truth about the pregnancy, but responded with a light-hearted and ultimately evasive joke. 'Well, there's a lot of problems,' he said when asked about Jolie's bump. 'Either it's a tremendous amount of gas, which is just not likely . . . Really, not likely.'

The more Jolie made the media wait for confirmation, the more hype surrounding the story snowballed, which was perhaps their intention. Soon reports insisted that yes, she was pregnant, but no, she wasn't expecting twins – just one child; a girl. Or was it a boy – the media couldn't get its story straight as reports emerged covering different scenarios. When Jolie reportedly collapsed during a flight, her friends were enormously concerned and the headlines bordered on hysterical. Finally, at the end of February, Jolie and Pitt began to confirm to those closest to them the wonderful truth: she was indeed expecting twins in the summer. They confided in pals, telling them the pregnancy wasn't planned but that they were both delighted – if a little overwhelmed – that two new additions to their growing brood were on the way. As these details began to find their way on to the printed page, there was an additional rumour that they would marry in the wake of the birth. Pitt, it was claimed, had finally convinced Jolie to tie the knot. 'It will be a strictly private affair,' claimed *Grazia* magazine. 'Brad did the big celebrity-packed wedding when he married Jennifer Aniston. This time it will be an intimate family gathering.' The wedding story proved to be nonsense, but it was true that they were expecting fraternal twins.

The news that they were expecting twins became official in a slightly unconventional fashion. Comedian

Jack Black joined Jolie for a live television interview to promote their film *Kung Fu Panda* and told Jolie, 'You will have as many as [the] Brady Bunch when you have these.' Since the famous television family had six children, this must mean that twins were on the way. 'It's confirmed?' asked the interviewer Natalie Morales, slightly surprised to be getting the scoop so effortlessly. 'Yeah, yeah, we've confirmed that already,' Jolie replied. 'Well, Jack's just confirmed it actually.' Morales got lucky again when she interviewed Dustin Hoffman at the Cannes Film Festival in May. Afterwards she told viewers, 'We were told by Dustin Hoffman in a separate interview that she [Jolie] is due on 19 August. It seems that everyone here is bursting at the seams with her breaking baby news.'

Jolie was enjoying her extra-large bump and boasted that it came with an unexpected benefit. 'It's great for the sex life,' she said. 'It makes you a lot more creative. So you have fun. And as a woman you're just so round and full.' They were also creative when it came to caring for their existing children. When one of the kids wanted to see their mom close up, Jolie would yell for Pitt, who would hand them to her to save her bending down. In April she felt the first kick of the pregnancy in rather unexpected surroundings. She was discussing Iraq education policy at the Council on Foreign Relations in Washington when it happened. '[I] felt kicking suddenly in the middle of the event,' she told *People* magazine. 'It's a very special time in our lives.' At home it seemed the only thing the couple argued about was political issues, or so Jolie said. One could be forgiven for thinking they were squabbling about everything if press reports were to be believed. Not true, she said – only current affairs. 'It's the only time we argue. A lot of time is spent arguing over things like justice. I am in favour of a harder line than he is.'

In May, Pitt was one of twelve guests who attended the forty-eighth birthday of rock star Bono. The select bash was held at Sass Café in Monaco, where Pitt and his fellow guests enjoyed a sit-down meal followed by a champagne toast and strawberry cake. The maître d' told *People* magazine, 'It was really quite a surprise. It wasn't organized in advance. We only got called on it that afternoon.' Among the other guests were Prince Albert of Monaco, Bono's wife Ali and U2 guitarist The Edge. Jolie had visited Bono in France the previous week, but didn't attend the party.

Soon, however, she, Pitt and the children would decamp to the south of France for the birth of the twins. Once again a media circus surrounded the story of the birth, and the couple's growing influence was recognized by a series of awards during 2008. In May Pitt was included in the esteemed Time 100. 'When a man looks like Brad Pitt, we tend to underestimate him,' read his listing. 'We ask him to make a block-buster a year. Date a beautiful woman. Have a cute baby. And we're happy. But he's not content. As an actor and producer, Pitt, 43, has used his star power to get people to look at places and stories that cameras don't usually catch.' It showed how his star was not only rising, but developing too as he became so much more than the pretty boy of his youth. The following month both he and Jolie were listed in *Forbes* magazine's Celebrity 100 list. Pitt came in at number five and Jolie at a respectable fourteenth place, but as a couple they came top of the *Forbes* 'most influential couple' poll. This was highly significant and showed once more that as a single entity their influence was far greater than as individuals. As for their fortune, this was hinted at when Jolie came a close second in the *Hollywood Reporter*'s list of best-paid actresses for 2007, which said that she demanded up to $20 million per movie.

As preparations for the birth of the twins began, Jolie was congratulated by her ex-husband Billy Bob Thornton. He had kind words for Pitt, too. 'I think she was always meant to be a mother in so many ways,' he said. 'I'm just so happy for her. I'm happy for the kids to have a mother like her and a father like him.' Pitt was not always as lucky when it came to ex-partners. Juliette Lewis had come back to haunt him several times and the shadow cast over his life by Aniston might not have been intentional on his ex-wife's part, but still showed no sign of disappearing. The same week as Thornton congratulated the couple, Aniston was said by the *National Enquirer* to be making disparaging remarks about Pitt's bedroom abilities compared to those of her current lover, musician John Mayer. 'Jennifer is calling John the best ever lover,' a source told the publication. 'In fact, she can't stop raving about his skills between the sheets.' It must have made uncomfortable reading for Pitt, but he and Jolie will have taken encouragement from the closing quote of the story. 'Only now, in John's arms, does she look even close to finally putting Pitt in the past tense,' claimed the source. How they hoped the source was right, and how the couple wished, as they packed their things and prepared to fly to the country where the twins would be born, that the public and press would leave Pitt and Aniston's marriage in the past. Not that there was much hope of that.

France had been chosen for the twins' birth partly in tribute to Jolie's late mother's French heritage. First they stayed at Villa Maryland, a breathtaking, £30-million Florentine-style palace on the French Riviera owned by Microsoft co-founder Paul Allen. With two helipads in the grounds, the couple had a military-trained pilot and a medical team on twenty-four-hour standby in case of emergencies. As we have seen, the couple could comfortably afford such vigilance, and it was a wise move given the health concerns Jolie was reported to have during pregnancy. There were reports of several episodes of fainting – two in mid-air during flights – which had caused alarm, as had Jolie's continued slender frame, despite her pregnant bump. It was also said that she was forced to wear oversized shoes – presumably to reduce the pain of her swollen feet – after being diagnosed with a form of diabetes that commonly strikes pregnant women. To complete the disturbing picture, it was reported that when the twins stopped kicking she had worried briefly that she'd lost them. Understandably, the couple were taking no chances as the due date approached, and were still coming to terms with the fact that they was expecting twins. 'We weren't expecting twins but we like a challenge,' said Jolie, adding that Pitt's parents were primed and ready to fly to France if needed after the birth.

Just as everyone had wanted the scoop on a Pitt-Jolie marriage, so reporters coveted the prospect of breaking the news about the twins' birth. On 31 May the US television show *Entertainment Tonight* confidently reported that Jolie had given birth to two baby daughters. Pitt's representative Cynthia Pett-Dante quickly rebutted the story in a statement: 'It's not true. It's a rumor.' However, *Entertainment Tonight* stood by its story, with host Mary Hart telling viewers, 'The source says she was inside the delivery room . . . the babies were born, and yes, mother and daughters are fine.' No such birth had taken place and no daughters had been born. The whirlwind surrounding the story continued and a bidding war for the first photographs of the babies was fierce, with fees of up to £8 million being mentioned by publications such as *People* and *OK!*, who were at the forefront of the auction. *OK!* were particularly keen, having missed out to British rivals *Hello!* when Shiloh was born, and the final total fee for the images would prove to be even higher than initially speculated.

In June, Pitt stayed at the Lake Como home of George Clooney, where he'd been rumoured to be marrying Jolie in 2007. This time he was crashing there, having attended a concert by one of his favourite rock bands, Radiohead. He had been to the concert with fellow actor Ed Norton and the widow of Daniel Pearl, who was the subject of *A Mighty Heart*, on one of his final big nights out before the twins arrived. At the beginning of June the preparations for the birth entered their final phase as Jolie was admitted to the Lenval Hospital in Nice. 'There's no urgency,' a hospital spokesperson told the swarming press. 'It's been planned for a long time. She's very well. Everything is fine.' Four separate rooms had been booked by the couple and the members of their medical entourage. Her obstetrician Dr Michel Sussmann reassured the world that the actress and her family were all in good health and spirits. 'Brad Pitt and Angelina Jolie have asked us to let you know that she's very well and she will give birth within the next few weeks,' he said as she was moved to the hospital. 'It isn't an emergency, it's completely planned. We're not talking about a premature birth. She's a pregnant woman and she's entitled to preserve her privacy. She will stay in the hospital as long as it takes, then she will be allowed to go home.'

A stringent level of security was put in place upon Jolie's arrival, but soon into her stay photographs were published claiming to show the interior of her accommodation. In the wake of their publication the hospital were quick to announce that it was 'impossible' that these photographs were authentic. 'Any pictures released are either posed fakes set up by paparazzi or they are pictures of other patients,' said a statement. 'We hope this is clearly understood out of respect for all patients in this clinic.' Finally, the news that everyone was waiting for came. When she had given birth to Shiloh via Caesarean section Angelina had found the experience 'a fascinating miracle of what a body can do'. Although there were plans for her to deliver the twins naturally, in the end she underwent another Caesarean on 12 July, giving birth to Knox Leon and Vivienne Marcheline, who weighed 5lb 3oz and 5lb respectively.

Sussman was quick to reassure the world of the twins' good health, announcing, 'The babies are doing well. The operation went just perfectly. Angelina is in very good spirits. Brad Pitt was at her side. He was there and all was well.' The doctor was in rather jovial mood as he expanded on the birth to the waiting reporters. He described Pitt as his 'assistant' during the procedure and said, 'He was perfectly calm, totally determined, very pleased to be at the birth of his children, very moved and very emotional.' When asked about the mother he said, 'It was an epidural, so she was awake and speaking and laughing. They were happy. She will stay for a few days. You know, in Europe it isn't like in the United States, where the patients go home after three days. They will stay a bit longer until everything is OK. The babies are fine. The babies are with the mother and father and they are fine.'

When the mother of the 'fine' babies first spoke she admitted she had been especially anxious about the birth because the babies arrived prematurely. 'So when I saw they were big and screaming with healthy lungs I was at peace,' she said. She wasn't the only one feeling anxious in the delivery room. Speaking to a European radio station later, Sussman admitted that his role in the delivery of two such globally anticipated babies had made him rather nervous. 'For sure,' he said. 'It wasn't pressure on a medical level, because I have been practising for a certain number of years, but it's true that there was pressure due to the couple's fame. I was assisted by a team that was totally competent, so things happened as I wanted them to happen – simply and efficiently.' Pitt remained focused and reassuring during what he was to chivalrously describe as an 'absolutely heroic' birth. He quickly noted distinguishing features between the two kids. 'I dare to say that Vivienne is proving to resemble Angelina in spirit,' he said of his new daughter. 'She is quite elegant like her mother. And Knox – he's a bit like me. He likes music like his dad. But when he was born he looked like [Russian President] Vladimir Putin!' Although Putin has at times been rated as one of the world's more ruggedly handsome leaders, it must have been a relief when Knox turned out to be more of a Pitt than a Putin.

A study of the couple's respective family trees reveals the inspiration for the babies' interesting names. Pitt's grandfather was called Hal Knox Hillhouse, while Angelina's great great grandfather was named Leon. His sister was named partly in honour of Jolie's late mother Marcheline, while the origin of the Vivienne part of the moniker is believed to be a reflection of the fact that she was born in France. Knox was almost named Rex, but according to reports the couple changed their minds at the last moment. Either name would have maintained their tradition of giving their boys names which end in 'x'. Having previously adopted children from different parts of the world and given birth to one child naturally, Jolie now had a new experience in looking after twins. It's a demanding task for a mother, but she was charmed by them from the very start. 'The twins are just the sweetest little things,' she beamed. 'They lay next to each other. The great thing about twins is how much company they are for each other. You see them together and they're looking at each other, they smell each other, they put their hands on each other and it's just beautiful to watch. You reach a point where you almost think that to have one baby alone would be kind of lonely. They're starting to smile a lot. Knox looks like Brad and Vivienne looks more like me. They are developing interesting personalities. Knox seems more relaxed and Vivienne is more loud.'

An interesting aspect of the press management of this particular birth is that the couple chose to hand the initial scoop not to an all-powerful publication such as *People*, *Hello!* or *Ok!*, but to a local French newspaper, *Nice-Matin*. Given the couple's influence and pulling power, they clearly made this decision to make a statement about press coverage and how they expected it to be conducted. The newspaper's editor Olivier Biscaye explained how and why he managed to get the scoop. 'It was Brad Pitt who chose to give the scoop to *Nice-Matin*. He said to the doctor that the local media should be the first informed about the birth. We knew we would be the first in the world. [Our reporter] spoke to the doctor . . . We had all the details: the names, weight, one boy, one girl. *Nice-Matin* has always chosen not to play the game of paparazzi towards the celebrities who have chosen to live in the region,' he explained. 'We respect them, and they do likewise. We let them have a peaceful life. This is why I think Brad and Angelina have chosen to make this gift to *Nice-Matin*.' How Pitt and Jolie must have wished the rest of the world's press was as considerate as *Nice-Matin*.

Once she and the twins were ready to leave hospital, Jolie managed to dodge the mass of reporters, photographers and cameramen by leaving at around 4.30 a.m. on a Saturday morning via the kitchen door. This helped keep the precious first photographs of the twins for a media auction, which was won by *People* magazine in America and *Hello!* in Britain in a combined $14 million deal. 'This is one of the publishing sensations of the decade,' said a magazine spokesperson. 'We expect to triple our circulation.' The couple announced they would be giving the enormous fee directly to charity.

Meanwhile the Pitt/Jolie collection of kiddies went from four to six overnight. Both were already experienced and widely praised parents, but twins presented a new set of challenges, not least at eating time. 'We try to get them to eat simultaneously for the sake of time management, but it gets a little crowded at the bar,' laughed the busy mother. She had hoped initially that it would be easier, but was in for a rude awakening. 'You think, "Ah, if anyone can do that, I can do that." But it's a lot harder than it looks in the books.' Speaking of jumping straight from four children to six, she concluded that after a while the numbers cease to matter. 'It's fun and it's lovely,' she said. 'The thing about having six kids is once you've passed three or four it's so crazy anyway that it's just more chaos and it's all OK.' They needed help to obtain some sense of control over the chaos and their famous friend, singer Wyclef Jean, was among those who offered to babysit to help take the pressure off. They were grateful for the offer and had an army of nannies and other staff already. The part of their lives that once again suffered in the wake of the twins' birth was grabbing time alone together for romantic moments. 'Even if we lock the door, the children still come knocking,' said Jolie. 'We often try to have a bath alone together at the end of the night and sit and talk, but they hear the water and want to jump in.'

For the moment the Jolie-Pitts were successfully transmitting an image of a happily chaotic household full of laughter and love, but trouble was not far down the road.

There was a further escalation of tension between

the couple and the press when their bodyguards scrapped with paparazzi the following week. Two photographers wearing camouflage outfits were discovered by bodyguards outside the couple's Chateau Miraval estate in France. The head of the security team, Tony Webb, said, 'We caught the two and tried to escort them off the property and the guy's just gone berserk, thrashing out, kicking and actually biting one of the security people, breaking his finger, drawing blood and screaming that he had Hepatitis C.' In the wake of the scrap, Voight spoke protectively and with concern about his daughter's plight in the face of such media intrusion. 'When you're just trying to do your daily chores and live your life and people are all over you trying to climb out of cars and windows, it's not so healthy,' he said. Since the death of Diana, Princess of Wales in 1997 there has been an extra sense of foreboding over the pressure put on celebrities by the more rapacious elements of the paparazzi. Jolie has often been compared with the late Diana and is said to be fascinated by her life.

Many celebrities claim not to be concerned about their media image, though the public tend not to believe them. In this media-savvy age, a cynicism has set in. Whatever you believe, though, there can be no doubt that some stars are more concerned with their image than others. Jennifer Aniston, for instance, has said, 'I just live my life, focus on my work and stick to the plan. I really don't worry about what's written about me.' Her words are easy to believe, at least in part, but Jolie has always appeared chronically concerned about her public image. In November *The New York Times* ran a feature entitled 'Angelina Jolie's Carefully Orchestrated Public Image'. It claimed that when negotiating with *People* for the rights to the first photographs of the twins and the first post-birth interview with her and Pitt, Jolie had suggested a number of conditions, including that the hated word 'Brangelina' would not be mentioned in the future and that the magazine would promise that the tone of the feature and future coverage would be favourable to the couple. Unnamed magazine sources insisted that the conditions had been requested, but *People* magazine firmly denied that they had been agreed to. 'These claims are categorically false,' the magazine said. 'Like any news organization, *People* does purchase photos, but the magazine does not determine editorial content based on the demands of outside parties.' Either way, the deal was a successful one for the magazine, which secured its best sales figures for seven years with the issue concerned.

The New York Times went on to portray Jolie as a woman obsessed with cultivating the exact image she wanted, and as an expert at making that happen. It made for a compelling argument, though no doubt Jolie would not have felt comfortable reading the article.

Indeed, if she is such a public relations wizard, one wonders why she sometimes makes public statements that at best seem ill-advised. A good example of this was when she revealed to *W* magazine that she had allowed her seven-year-old son Maddox to accompany her shopping for knives. 'We take him to a special shop,' said the woman who self-harmed as a youngster. 'We also talk about samurais and the idea about defending someone as good. We talk about everything.' Just how contentious this revelation was can be measured by the fact that it drew condemnation from controversial reality TV star Kerry Katona of all people. 'My daughter Molly is the same age and I would never even think about doing the same,' said Katona. 'I hate knives.' When you're attracting moral censure from someone as colourful and controversial as Katona, it is perhaps time to take stock.

Jolie and Pitt have both been warmly praised by those who've seen their parenting skills up close. However, people in the wider world were beginning to wonder whether Jolie would be able to cope with the pressure of bringing up six children, and in the wake of the twins' birth, journals across the world were peppered with suggestions that she was struggling. The *Sydney Morning Herald* said she feared that her children might be kidnapped. Soon *Star* magazine claimed that Pitt was encouraging Jolie to see a therapist, while in a separate article, television celebrity Ulrika Jonsson wondered how Jolie managed to cope with such demands. 'I know what the demands of having four children are,' she told *Hello!* 'But six – in such a short space of time . . . I sometimes wonder if she's given herself a chance to adapt.' So how were they managing? Speaking at the Toronto Film Festival, where he was promoting *Burn After Reading*, Pitt would only admit that the couple were longing for the chance to get some 'healthy sleep'. An unnamed source backed this up when they told *Life&Style* magazine, 'Sometimes he's so tired he can barely speak.'

While he was in Toronto, Pitt was evacuated from his hotel after a fire broke out in a seventh-floor condo. Nobody was hurt but the scene as he was rushed out of the building made great theatre for onlookers. 'It was total chaos,' said an eyewitness. 'His security team immediately decided to evacuate Brad to avoid any possible threat. He was surrounded by eight security men and four policemen – it was crazy. It was as if Brad was the president!' The irony that he was in town to promote a film called *Burn After Reading* wasn't lost on Pitt. He was also jostled when he attended the film premiere of *The Curious Case of Benjamin Button* in November – but by his own security. Photographers were snapping him when his security team intervened. According to one of the photographers, Pitt was manhandled by his own bodyguards during the scuffle, though Pitt was philosophical about the episode. 'Though they were exceptionally more aggressive than usual, breaking through a security barrier and into a private holding area, ultimately [it was] just another day in the life,' he said.

Both Pitt and Jolie enjoy close friendships with many of their fellow celebrities. However, in such a keenly competitive business there are often tensions and spats, both behind the scenes and in public. In September Pitt and his old pal George Clooney both wanted the role of Henry Higgins in a remake of *My Fair Lady*. 'We both badly want a particular role and neither is backing down,' Clooney said, according to *OK!* magazine. 'It's sort of become an intense competition between us now and it just keeps escalating.' He claimed that the tension had reached the point where the pair were no longer speaking. If things ever did get that bad, the disagreement must have been quickly resolved as the two remain good friends. The chances of warm relations developing between Jolie and actress/comedienne Roseanne Barr are slim, however, after Barr wrote a post on her website addressed to Jolie's father. 'Your evil spawn Angelina Jolie and her vacuous hubby Brad Pitt make about $40 million a year in violent, psychopathic movies and give away three of it to starving children, trying to look as if they give a crap about humanity as they spit out more dunces that will consume more than their fair share and wreck the earth even more,' Barr wrote venomously. Concluding the post, she addressed Jolie directly, 'Now go back to making your movies about women who love to handle big guns that shoot hundreds of people to death.'

Such professional criticism was hurtful, even for Jolie, who had developed a thick skin after so many years in the public eye and all the knocks that come with a high-profile life. In any case, she was more concerned at this stage with managing the comments about her relationship, and both she and Pitt continued to put on a united front to a doubting world. She insisted that far from losing interest in her sexually since the birth of their children, Pitt had come to appreciate her body more as it developed as a result of pregnancy and birth. 'He genuinely sees it that way,' she said and, warming to her theme, she once more painted a picture of a happy household. 'I genuinely feel even sexier. I am fortunate enough to live with my favourite people in the world, including Brad, who is my best friend and an amazing father. Our life is very, very hard work, but it's also a lot of fun. We have each other and we have a lot of love in our life. And anybody who has love in their life has something that is much more important than anything else.' She said that her six children were getting on well, too, with the older siblings taking a caring role towards the newer arrivals to the clan. 'It's so much fun but it's very hard work. The kids are forming beautiful friendships. They're teammates and they're very loving to the babies.'

These images were enough to warm the hearts of even the most icy cynics, but the iciest of the lot – celebrity journalists – would take a whole lot more convincing. They continued to insist that things were far from well behind the scenes in the Brangelina household.

In the middle of September a rumour spread like wildfire across the internet that Pitt and Jolie had separated. Although the mainstream media has always loved speculating about the state of the couple's relationship, its outlets can – to a degree at least – be controlled by clever press management and the laws of libel. However, the internet is a Wild West for unsubstantiated rumours, and the story spread fast. Jolie's spokesperson slammed the gossip, stating, 'The stories are absolutely not true.' Far from the family falling apart, the camp insisted, it would become bigger before long. Jolie was unabashed by the speculation and told the *Today* show that she and Pitt already had plans to add to their family. She said they would return to the adoption route. 'You can't even start the process until any new children are six months old, to understand how the new family has settled,' she said. 'We have so many children that they're not really stunned any more when kids come home.' Then, speaking at the release party for the DVD of *Kung Fu*

Panda, she said of Pitt, 'He's the best daddy and we have fun, so whenever it gets hard we can just look at each other and find a way to laugh and just appreciate that they're only little once, and we should enjoy every minute. We're open to anything, we love kids and we're having a great time . . . It's chaos in our house, but it's so much fun. We'll definitely have more.' However, reports that she was pregnant with a fourth biological child were quickly dismissed. She continued to speak in such cute terms about her children that it was easy to believe she was feeling broody. 'They're great,' she glowed. 'They're still so little, but they do have their own personalities. They are starting to get very smiley, and they are at those months where their personalities really start to shine,' she added.

As Christmas approached, Pitt was in upbeat mode during a personal interview with *Hello!* magazine. Despite their multi-million-dollar fortune, the parents insisted that for the festive season the family should not buy each other presents but make each other something instead. 'The rule is that everyone's got to make something for someone else, you got to put your time into it,' he told the magazine. 'Then when they give to each other, it's really sweet.' He explained that he and their mother restricted the amount of television the children were allowed to watch, in part to avoid them seeing the 'manipulative' advertisements for expensive toys that flood the airwaves in

November and December. 'When they do see that stuff is when they start asking for the toys, so we figure if they don't see them they won't know they're there,' he said. While not necessarily doubting the veracity of his words it must be observed that this is Brangelina spin at its best: painting a picture of a happy wholesome family and casting the wildly successful and fabulously wealthy couple in a more liberal and relaxed light.

The Jolie-Pitt family had swelled to eight members in total, and though they still hadn't married – rumours that they wed in New Orleans were dismissed as 'complete and total bullshit' – they were still together, contrary to the expectations and predictions of many. There had been a concerted effort by both Pitt and Jolie to present a united front to the doubtful but ever fascinated world. Had they done enough to dispel the doubts of those who believed that beneath the happy exterior theirs was an unhappy relationship? Not a bit of it. The celebrity press was as obsessed as ever with their relationship, and just as hungry to break stories about its demise. Meanwhile, increasingly they attempted to conjure up the prospect of a reunion between Pitt and his ex-wife Jennifer Aniston. The media simply refused to allow the pair to move on from one another, and although Aniston had been largely serene about their split, she changed her tune in November 2008. 'What Angelina did was very uncool,' she told *Vogue*.

Had Pitt and Jolie's relationship been a movie, this would be the perfect point at which to reintroduce the character of Aniston into a key role following a period of sporadic cameo appearances. She was, after all, the dashing damsel that many viewers wanted to see returned to Pitt's side. Such a fantasy plot inevitably casts Jolie as the de facto baddie, but in real life none of their roles was as neat as that. Armchair directors across the globe were conjuring the end of Brangelina in their minds, and real-life editors everywhere were preparing to shout, 'Action!'

10. The End?

The eye of the storm might be the calmest part, but it's not without its hazards and tribulations. Recent months have been stormy for Pitt and Jolie as the world wondered whether the most famous celebrity relationship of the moment – and perhaps the most powerful couple 'brand' of all time – was about to come undone. With Pitt now comfortably into his forties, but Jolie still in her mid-thirties, it's reasonable to speculate that their outlooks on life will become increasingly different over the next few years. Add into this mix that Pitt has always been considered a calmer character, more inherently attracted to the idea of settling down, and that Jolie has – largely by her own public admission – always been the more volatile character with burning social ambitions, and one wonders if their futures ultimately lie apart.

As speculation about his present and future grew, Pitt chose to make a statement about the past. It was the perception that he had cheated on Aniston with Jolie during the making of *Mr. & Mrs. Smith* that made the public cynical about his sincerity in general, so he denied once again that he had ever been disloyal to

Aniston during their marriage. He said firmly that there was no 'dastardly affair. There wasn't. I'm very proud of the way it was handled. It was respectful'. He added that suggestions of an ongoing feud between Aniston and Jolie were also wide of the mark. He did, however, admit that he was still in touch with his ex-wife. 'Jen and I still check in with each other,' he said. 'She was a big part of my life, and me hers. I don't see how there cannot be that. That's life, man. That's life.' Within months of this statement reports alleged that he was close to a reunion with Aniston.

Jolie chose to focus on the present and shrugged off rumours of discord in the household by emphasizing the positives, although one of the words she used during her glowing tribute was eagerly seized upon by observant cynics. 'We are a good team,' she said. The following month she said of her older partner, '[Brad's] taught me a great deal. He's a wonderful man and a great father and the person I admire most in the world because I know who he is every minute of every day,' she said. 'I think he's extraordinary . . . We've been doing [the red carpet] together for four years – it's always nice [to have him around]. I don't think I'd want to be doing it alone. It's nice to be doing it with your best friend and have a laugh in the middle of the show.' Those with good memories will recall that it was shortly after Pitt and Aniston began referring to themselves as 'friends' that their marriage broke down. Could Jolie's less than romantic description, during an interview with the German edition of *Cosmopolitan*, signify a similar fate for them? Had the couple who had long been rumoured to have a wild and passionate sex life have fallen out of lust with one another?

Pitt might be in his forties, but for many women he still remains a dream catch. It is believed that – physically at least – Pitt and Jolie's love remains strong. Except for on one occasion, as the couple readily admit. Pitt surprised some when he revealed that Jolie rarely watches the films he appears in. Speaking of the film *Burn After Reading*, he told *Newsweek*, 'She has seen that one. In fact, it's probably the only one she's seen. She walked on set and I was in the gym gear and the hair, and she said, "This is the first time I can honestly say I'm not sexually attracted to you in any way whatsoever".' To listen to some in the industry the very opposite is normally the problem. Chauffeurs speak of how lustful they can be, even in the back seat of a car, and Pitt's co-star in *The Curious Case of Benjamin Button*, Cate Blanchett, joked during an interview with the *Daily Telegraph* that she would never work with Pitt again because he was too 'loved up' with Jolie. 'Honestly, to see how in love with Angelina he is, it was really quite disgusting. Awful in fact. It's in my contract now: I won't ever work with him again.' Blanchett's words might have been meant humorously, but they certainly painted a romantic image of the couple.

Pitt admitted that working on *The Curious Case of Benjamin Button* had given him a new perspective on life. 'I walked away realizing that time is short. I don't know if I have a day or ten days or ten years or forty years. Am I halfway or am I close to the end?' he said. 'I don't know, so I have to make sure I don't waste those moments in any kind of pettiness or bitterness or laziness, and that I surround myself with the people who are most important to me.' One is reminded of the car crash he was involved in as a student and the sudden perspective that gave him on the fragility of life. In the wake of that incident he had walked away from his journalism studies, even though he was about to graduate after years of effort. Now he was talking about death. 'I'm not so afraid of getting old, I'm more afraid of how I'll go. Fire and tight spaces don't appeal. A shark would be interesting.' It was assumed that 'the people who are most important' to him would be Jolie and his six children, but all this talk of perspective couldn't help but set tongues wagging and minds speculating again. Indeed, it seemed that there was nothing Pitt and Jolie could do or say which wouldn't be spun by some part of the media as evidence of their impending break-up.

Rumours of infidelities abounded but were never

confirmed by the couple. However, the nature of their exclusivity to one another was clarified by Jolie during an interview with the *Daily Telegraph*. It was Jolie – painted as a tempestuous and possessive character – who wanted to maintain monogamy. But if this had ever been her stance, then by 2009 it had changed. 'I doubt that fidelity is absolutely essential for a relationship. It's worse to leave your partner and talk badly about him afterwards,' she told the British newspaper. 'Neither Brad nor I have ever claimed that living together means to be chained together. We make sure that we never restrict each other.' There had been a stream of stories that she and Pitt were squabbling and Jolie was honest about these too. 'The sparks fly at home if the nice Brad fails to see that he's wrong and reacts in a defiant way,' she said. 'Then I can get so angry that I tear his shirt.' When he was promoting *The Curious Case of Benjamin Button* in Germany, Pitt was reported to have got into hot water with Jolie after partying into the early hours at Kaisersaal. Jolie was said to have read him the riot act when he came back to their hotel at 2 a.m. after she had headed home earlier so that she could get enough rest to perform the early-morning feeding shift for the children. Unnamed insiders were quoted by *In Touch Weekly* claiming that Pitt 'misses his carefree, kid-free days – so he sneaks away for solo nights of drinking to recapture his youth'. Next time he was asked publicly about his partying he seemed chastened, saying, 'I am a father – my partying ends at 6 p.m.'

During 2009 Pitt grew a goatee beard that drew comments aplenty at office water coolers around the world. What was this pin-up doing cultivating a 'hobo' look? It was originally believed to be in preparation for a film role, but this has since been discounted. When he was at the Golden Globes after-party in January he received some feedback about the controversial growth. A drunken woman approached him to tell him how ugly he had looked in *The Curious Case of Benjamin Button*, and her parting shot – to the amusement of Pitt's friends, who were sitting with him – was to say, 'And you should definitely shave that goatee because it looks just horrible.' Was the former pin-up's popularity with the ladies waning? Not entirely, according to some polls, as in May he came fourth in a poll about the best celebrity hairstyles. A leading Hollywood plastic surgeon had more heartening news for the couple when he revealed that his clients regularly wanted to look like them, with 'give me Angelina Jolie lips' being a regular request. How far the stunning actress had come since her school days, when she was teased and bullied for her fulsome lips. However, *Now* magazine claimed that Jolie had told people close to her that she was unhappy with the sags and wrinkles that had appeared on her body since giving birth to the twins.

When she was filming the espionage film *Salt*, Jolie cut an isolated and tired figure – it wasn't a look that anyone who flicks religiously through the pages of celebrity magazines would ever aspire to. 'Brad and the kids have barely visited the set and Angelina seems very insular,' an insider told the *Mail on Sunday*. 'She's staying on her own, working fifteen-hour days and the stress is taking its toll. We're all very concerned. She is looking so small on camera, the producers have had to have a discreet word.' As filming continued she was said to have collapsed on set, with sources telling the *Chicago Sun-Times* that she complained of breathlessness and a dizzy feeling before falling to the ground. Within weeks there were rumours that Jolie was ready to adopt another child, this time from the Philippines, though this has never materialized. The family did visit Long Island, however, where they caused a stir by visiting a local store. 'It's the big buzz of the town,' said the delighted store owner. 'We have had celebrities in before and it's exciting, but these are the most famous people in the world.' It was a reminder that for all the doubts about their relationship, together they remained a potent celebrity force.

For how long, though, would they want to maintain their film work and the fame that comes with it? Jolie says that her film work comes fourth on her list of priorities, after being a mother, her relationship with Pitt and her charity work. During a thoughtful interview with *Newsweek* magazine Pitt hinted that he was tired of the publicity demands that customarily come with working on a big movie. 'It's everything we didn't sign up for,' he said. 'There's this whole other entity that you get sucked into. You have to go and sell your wares. It's something I never made my peace with. Somehow you're not supporting your film if you don't get out on a show and talk about your personal life. It has nothing to do with why I do this. I feel for the people who are just getting into the business. It sets the wrong focus.' During just such a promotional 'junket' for his world war two film *Inglourious Basterds*, he told NBC's *Today* show that he was happy in his life and relationship with Jolie. 'Let me be the cliché, it's really rewarding,' he said. 'It's really been about discovery and finding new things of interest. And the kids are certainly responsible for a lot of that.' When asked if he was experiencing the happiest time of his life so far, Pitt said he was 'right in the zone' and that it is 'one of the most on-track times'. He added, 'I'm really proud of this family. I look at my sons and daughters . . . I feel rich being around them. Each one offers so much to the mix.' Pitt was then asked if he and Jolie would ever tie the knot. 'If we feel it's important to our kids we would,' was his reply. However, the agenda for coverage of their relationship from now on would focus not on predicting a marriage, as it had done for so long. Now the world's editors wanted just one story: that Pitt and Jolie had split up.

It was while his ex-wife Aniston was on the publicity trail for her latest film *He's Just Not That Into You* that she made a revelation to *Marie Claire* magazine that fed speculation and gave credence to the idea that she was still into Pitt. She confessed to keeping voice messages from her old flames, including Pitt. 'I still have the cassette tapes of messages from my first boyfriend, my second boyfriend, my husband . . . it's like saving love letters,' she said. The same week that her admission grabbed the headlines, stories emerged that Jolie was planning another pregnancy, and on a separate occasion she told a television interviewer that she was the 'happiest mummy'. From here on the news reports would 'see-saw' between 'Brangelina are on the rocks' and 'All is well with Brangelina'. As one report cast doubts on Pitt and Jolie's happiness, so another would reinforce it, leaving all those involved feeling dizzy after a while.

Aniston was in loquacious mood again later that month during an interview with the *News of the World*. Once more the topic of Pitt was firmly on the agenda. 'I really thought I'd be with him for the rest of my life,' she admitted. 'It was a beautiful, complicated relationship. The sad thing, for me, is the way it's been reduced to a Hollywood cliché. But I don't regret any of it. The marriage didn't work out, but pretty soon after we separated, we got on the phone and we had a long, long conversation and said a lot of things. And ever since we've been unbelievably warm and respectful of each other.' She was at this stage dating musician John Mayer, but her remarks about Pitt did nothing to help the perception of his current relationship.

The Curious Case of Benjamin Button and *He's Just Not That Into You* were released at the same time, prompting interest in whether Pitt's or Aniston's film would do best at the box office. Pitt was the winner in the UK, with *Benjamin Button* taking £2,213,495 in the first week of release compared to *He's Just Not That Into You*'s £1,913,542. When *Forbes* released its influential annual top ten of Hollywood's most bankable stars that year, neither Pitt nor Jolie topped the list, or even managed the top three. Will Smith came top and Jolie came fourth, ahead of Pitt in fifth place, and between them and the top spot were Johnny Depp and Leonardo DiCaprio.

In February the couple attended the BAFTA awards in London hand in hand while a nanny looked after their four eldest children, who were back at the family's hotel, the Dorchester on Park Lane. According to the *Sun* newspaper the kids began to 'run amok' at the hotel, forcing Pitt and Jolie to leave early to take control of the situation. The next awards ceremony they attended was the Oscars in Los Angeles, where they were nominated in the best actor and actress categories for their respective parts in *The Curious Case of Benjamin Button* and *Changeling*. Ahead of the Oscars they were on opposite coasts of America, with Jolie spotted shopping with her daughters Shiloh and Zahara in New York while Pitt was out and about in Las Vegas with sons Maddox and Pax Thien. At the Oscars they both missed out on an award, with the best actress Oscar going to Kate Winslet for *The Reader* and best actor being won by Sean Penn for *Milk*. In the wake of the ceremony an enterprising deodorant brand sent Pitt a chocolate Oscar trophy saying, 'We still feel your performance deserves a statue, one that's a bit sweeter.' It was nice, but ultimately scant consolation. The same narrative that was casting Aniston as the good girl and Jolie as the baddie placed Pitt in a more favourable light. Comic actor Jim Carrey comically referred to the sometimes lopsided media attitudes to Jolie during an interview on an American talk show. 'Well you really can't say anything about Brad Pitt. Angelina Jolie? Oh yeah, so she's the problem for sure, we're okay with him, seriously, because he can do no wrong.'

Aniston meanwhile was in all senses at the top of her game: she looked fantastic and her career was going great guns, with four films scheduled during

2010 and 2011. She was also getting plenty of attention from handsome, famous men, including – according to reports – pin-up actor Jake Gyllenhaal and model Paul Sculfor. Indeed, she was so popular that, she remarked, even her dog Norman was recognized in public as a celebrity mutt. Aniston no longer appeared the spurned, upset ex-wife meeting up with her former love, but rather a successful, happy woman who could show she didn't need him. As such, she must have seemed even more of a pull. As *Now* magazine put it, Aniston was 'always the loser, she's now got the upper hand'. Aniston clearly decided she needed to create a bigger distance between herself and Pitt. The media still tried to engineer stories of a romantic reunion. In many ways this would have been the perfect happy-ever-after to the plot. But not for Aniston, at least not if she listened to her friends. Her yoga teacher Mandy Ingber told her, 'Any man would be lucky to have you,' and singer Sheryl Crow echoed this theme, telling her friend, 'Look at all the great guys you've recently dated – you're hot stuff!' Actress Courteney Cox is a longstanding friend of Aniston's who spoke for all the former *Friends* star's pals when she said, 'We just want the best for you – don't get involved in any drama.' Television megastar Oprah Winfrey hoped for the best for Aniston, too, and said, 'Don't rush into anything, or risk getting your heart broken again.'

This wave of sympathy for Aniston had an impact on Jolie, too, who, during 2009 and 2010, reportedly received a volley of hate mail and menacing threats from Aniston fans. While there was no suggestion that Aniston was in any way involved with this abuse, the story underlined how much the standing of both actresses had changed since 2005 when Pitt moved from one to the other. 'As Angelina's beauty fades . . . Jen looks better than ever,' trumpeted *Heat* magazine in February. Aniston did indeed look amazing when she arrived at the Golden Globes ceremony in a breathtaking black Valentino dress. And on accepting her gong for her contribution to film at the Crystal and Lucy Awards in Los Angeles she made the audience laugh with a pertinent and witty observation. She joked, 'I have a strange parallel with movies I do and my life off screen. First, it was *The Good Girl* . . . which evolved into *Rumor Has It*, followed by *Derailed*. Then there was *The Break-Up*. Followed by the lighter side, *Friends With Money*. If anyone has a movie called *Everlasting Love With an Adult Stable Man* that would be great!' As the audience laughed, it seemed that it was Aniston who was having the last laugh when it came to her split with Pitt.

As Aniston's star continued to shine more brightly a darker cloud was hanging over Pitt and Jolie – at least if you believe what you read in the newspapers. All they could do was keep countering the stories, as

Pitt did when he told the *Mirror*, 'I am in love and I have the most beautiful family – what else can a guy want?' That year he was also inducted into the Guy Hall of Fame by Spike TV in June, being handed the honour by controversial film star Mel Gibson, who in 2006 was arrested for drink driving and reportedly told a female officer, 'Thanks, sugar tits.' When Pitt arrived on stage at the ceremony he shook Gibson's hand and said, 'Thanks, sugar tits,' to raucous laughter. It was a proud evening for Pitt, but it was Jolie who would receive the most profound and significant honour. In the first week of June she was named top of the Forbes Celebrity 100 list. Oprah Winfrey had been the most powerful celebrity in the world for the last two years, but now it was time for Jolie to knock Oprah off her perch and claim top spot. Forbes senior editor Matthew Miller said, 'In addition to nearly doubling her earnings in the past year, from £9 million to £16 million, Angelina Jolie is the most famous star on the planet. She is in the dialogue of popular culture nearly every day – for her acting, for her relationship with Brad Pitt, for her children and for her philanthropic endeavours. All of this exposure leads to an extremely powerful celebrity brand – one that allows her to command a higher salary when starring in movies, can bring more people to the theatre and one that she can monetise further if she chose to do so.' It was a vindicating moment for her. Let the headline-writers speculate and the general public criticize her all they liked, Jolie's star was on the rise. Pitt finished in ninth place, behind his ex-wife Jennifer Aniston. When Forbes listed the top 10 earning actors between June 2008 and June 2009, Pitt came eighth, with an estimated income of £18.6 million.

But might his high-earning, all-powerful partner be ready to retire from acting? She had been discussing such a move for four years. In 2005 and 2007 she had foreshadowed her retirement, but each time went on to sign up for more films. Then in October 2008 she reprised the theme, telling *Vanity Fair*, 'The kids are my priority, so it's possible that from now on I will make fewer movies. I may even stop altogether.' More recently she has claimed that both she and Pitt will only take on one film a year in order to spend more time with their children, though their schedules in recent years have contradicted this. Different theories abound as to why Jolie regularly makes but never keeps her vows to retire. Could it be that she's hoping to raise her fees for future films by appearing reluctant to take part in them? Another theory is that she's addicted to work and wants to quit but cannot bring herself to do so. She admitted as much during an interview in 2000. Sources in the movie world speculate that perhaps she keeps mentioning retirement as a public relations effort to fend off suggestions that she's too focused on work to look after her children properly, though such suggestions seem unfair, as even Jolie's biggest critics accept that she and Pitt are great parents. They have to be in order to keep up with the demands of six kids while remaining happy. 'I run around with all the kids so it's pretty busy,' said Jolie. 'But I feel great and I am very happy that they're healthy.'

Days later the *National Enquirer* said that Pitt and Jolie were on the brink of announcing an 'official split'. It was a sensational story that was quickly denied by Pitt's representatives as 'absolutely not true', while Jolie's spokesperson branded the claim 'not true at all'. At the end of the week the *Sunday Mirror* reported that, far from being on the point of breaking up, the couple were planning to marry. 'Usually it's Brad who wants to talk marriage. But this time it was Angelina. An aide sent them all the clippings about their relationship problems and Angelina said it was probably best if they married and put an end to the speculation. Brad's face lit up, he was thrilled. He definitely wants to get married before they have any more babies. He needs to know Angelina is really committed to him. Becoming Mrs Pitt would give him that answer.'

Once again the wedding never materialized, but the report was enough to quell rumours of a split – for a while at least. Rumours that the couple were house-hunting together in Manhattan added to the happy family picture, as did the family party they held in Los Angeles to celebrate the twins' first birthday. It wasn't long, though, until new rumours of discord surfaced. It was claimed that after a heated row with Pitt, Jolie had stormed out of their home. 'Minutes after the argument, she got up, threw together a bag of clothes and ran to her car,' a source told *Grazia* magazine. 'She checked straight into a suite at the Raffles L'Ermitage hotel.' Among the topics that the couple are rumoured to argue about are where they will be buried when they die and what food to feed the children. On the latter subject Pitt is said to favour a vegetarian diet for the kids, partly due to his concerns over the damage done by methane gases from cattle.

Such was life in the eye of the storm. Earlier in his career Pitt had found wild speculation about his private life very upsetting and difficult to deal with. He told *The Times* newspaper that he had since learned to cope with it and insisted that he and Jolie were not behind any of the unattributed stories that regularly appear about them in the press. 'We just don't really participate,' he said. 'It kind of goes on without us. It's self-generating. When I was younger I would take it personally; it was such an injustice to me. As a man or as a woman I don't know how they could sit there and do it. I mean, [the stories] are consciously fabricated and I don't know how you could do that.'

Earlier in the year a report had claimed that Jolie had caught Pitt rubbing their nanny's back after she had been taken ill. A source close to Pitt later told *Hello!* magazine that the rumour was not just untrue but 'probably the dumbest story of all'. The insider added, 'Like Brad would do such a thing. He might not want me to say so, but that really p***ed him off. It made him sound so empty-headed and foolhardy, and that is so not who he is. But this is what happens when they're not always out there in the public eye. People make up stories about them just to keep them in the news.'

Jolie's reported interest in the life of Diana, Princess of Wales, reminds us that celebrity and tragedy are familiar bedfellows. While her death in 1997 shook the world, there had long been an air of tragedy around the princess, and a sense of inevitability that her life would end abruptly and prematurely. The same could be said of other famous deaths in recent times, such as that of pop legend Michael Jackson. Then there are those stars who have been assassinated at a young age, such as Beatle John Lennon and fashion designer Gianni Versace. Even the seemingly wholesome can die young, such as Boyzone singer Stephen Gately. Of course, ordinary 'civilian' people sometimes die in high-speed car accidents, drug-fuelled disasters or even shootings, but fame seems to attract a disproportionate number of horrific endings. Jolie has in many ways lived life on the edge, even though recently she appears to have become a calmer woman who is praised for her mothering ways. One hopes she can therefore dodge the morbid curse that seems to grip the world of celebrity.

In more positive news it was revealed that Pitt's brother Doug had handed a $1 million cheque on behalf of the couple to St John's Hospital in Springfield, Missouri. It would help fund a new cancer unit, which was to be named the Jane Pitt Pediatric Cancer Center, after the actor's mother. The Jolie-Pitt Foundation then pledged an identical sum to helping Pakistani refugees. On World Refugee Day Jolie spoke out to deny that she was political. While making a high-profile visit to Iraq in the summer, the couple spoke to the press at a refugee camp. 'This is a moment where things seem to be improving on the ground, but Iraqis need a lot of support and help to rebuild their lives,' said Jolie. 'The picture in this camp is a rough one, but there are also some people that were able to return home to other safer areas. There are some changes.' She told the residents of the camp that she hoped the next time she saw them their lives would have improved. Elsewhere in 2009 she denied that her tireless work for humanitarian causes was overtly political. 'I'm not a political person,' she said. 'But I think it doesn't take much to understand that this is the frontline of us fighting against extremists where . . . all that we hold dear and all that we value is really on the line. This fight is a very personal fight for all of us.'

In a similar clarifying statement Pitt was keen to make clear that he was no longer religious. The man who was brought up as a Southern Baptist said, 'I'm probably 20 per cent atheist and 80 per cent agnostic. I don't think anyone really knows. You'll either find out or not when you get there, until then there's no point thinking about it.' He later added that after his statements in support of gay marriage he had been astounded to face attacks for his stance from religious leaders. 'I took a lot of flak for saying it – hate mail from religious groups,' he said. 'Just the other night, I heard this TV reverend say that Angie and I were setting a bad example because we were living out of wedlock, and people should not be duped by us! It made me laugh. What damn right does anyone have to tell someone else how to live if they're not hurting anyone?' The same week he gave an interview to *Parade* magazine, and it's unlikely that much of what he said went down well in the religious community. He boasted that he and Jolie enjoyed having al fresco romps in their garden and also spoke about the reasons why he had first moved out of Hollywood. 'I liked to smoke a bit of grass at the time, and I became very sheltered,' he said. 'Then I got bored. I was turning into a damn doughnut, really. So I moved as far away from that as I could. I was done.' The Baptist community he grew up in must have been horrified by what had become of the wholesome, boyish young man who sang in church each Sunday.

Given that Jolie had claimed that she and Pitt made sure not to 'restrict' one another, people wondered whether Jolie enjoyed any same-sex extracurricular activities. Television host Rosie O'Donnell, who came out as a lesbian in 2002, claimed in a television interview with Howard Stern that Jolie and her had once discussed a possible date. 'She gave me her phone number,' she said, speaking of the period between Jolie's relationships with Thornton and Pitt. 'We talked on the phone two or three times, but that was that . . . There was a tentative plan to have dinner that never came through. I was a little afraid of her. She's scary in a sexual kind of way. I have dreams about her a lot still.'

On Halloween Jolie cut a scary figure as she joined Pitt and the kids for some trick-or-treating in the Hollywood hills, having powdered her face white and slapped fake blood on her forehead. Daughter Zahara was dressed in a Batman costume and eight-year-old Maddox wore a camouflage outfit, with Shiloh clad in a similar military outfit. Pitt, meanwhile, was decked out in a bright orange outfit with beads in his beard in tribute to DJ Lance Rock, a character from the children's TV show *Yo Gabba Gabba!* The DJ later said he thought the actor looked 'awesome' in the costume. It was a happy night for all the family and one in which they managed to have some semblance of normality. It was a different story just weeks earlier, though, when Pitt had fallen off his motorbike in Los Angeles. He was unhurt in the incident and subsequently blamed it on a paparazzo, who he claimed tried to block his path. 'I had a little mishap,' he said. 'No injuries, except my ego. I was trying to get away from some paparazzi and instead gave them a good story. It was my favourite bike, so that is really sad.' In the end he resolved to purchase a new vehicle while he was in Japan promoting *Inglourious Basterds.*

While one relationship was said to be on the rocks, however, two related ones were resurrected in 2009. In May Aniston began to forgive her mother for her past indiscretions. 'Things are now fine between us,' she said, according to the *New York Post.* 'All of that is over, and we're in touch with one another. Today Mum has moved from California and she's living in Colorado, and we speak. It's all over.' Then, in the autumn, Jolie and her father began to speak again after many years of estrangement. Speaking to *Us Weekly,* Voight said, 'We're in touch, but not regularly. We love each other and that's the most important thing.' Jolie too confirmed that they were tentatively in touch, telling *Stylist* magazine that she and her father were 'in contact now and writing letters'.

The Museum of Contemporary Art marked its thirtieth anniversary with a bash to launch a special exhibition in Los Angeles. It was a star-studded event with a guest list including Gwen Stefani, Gavin Rossdale, Christina Ricci, Jessica Alba, Kate Beckinsale, Guy Ritchie, James Franco, Pierce Brosnan and Lady Gaga. However, all talk on the night was about two people, Pitt and Jolie. So intense had speculation become about their relationship that any public outing they made together received unprecedented levels of attention. A few weeks later they were seen dining in Beverly Hills with George Clooney and a female companion, and an eyewitness told the press the couple looked 'surprisingly happy'. Whether intentional or not, the pictures promoted as blissful an image as possible. It was claimed that Pitt had turned down a lucrative offer of £3 million for a simple personal appearance in Dubai in order to go on the aforementioned family trick-or-treating outing. Meanwhile *Showbiz Spy* reported that Jolie too planned to decrease her professional activities in favour of domestic ones. 'I am just a mum and that's how I'm going to be the rest of my life,' she said. 'That sounds so funny, I mean, A-list actor. I am so happy to be working as an actor and to take some time off whenever I can, and that's something not a lot of people can do. I am so fortunate to juggle both.'

At the turn of the decade countless awards were given to mark the past ten years. One of them, by cosmetics retailer Superdrug, was for the most beautiful woman of the decade. The winner was Angelina Jolie, who finished ahead of her supposed rival Jennifer Aniston. 'Jolie is not a conventional beauty, but her strong character shines through her fabulous features to give her a unique standing in the beauty world,' said the retailer's commercial director Steve Jebsen. 'It's worth noting that while everyone talks about Angelina's pout, we find that it's her long thick lustrous hair that really makes women envious, as well as a figure made for red carpet posturing.'

Speaking of hair, Pitt continued to grow an extraordinarily lengthy goatee that drew comparisons with everyone from ZZ Top to the homeless. As *Forbes* magazine placed Pitt and Jolie as the third highest-earning couple (top ranking now went to rapper Jay-Z and singer Beyoncé) the break-up rumours continued.

The irritating drip-drip of stories about the couple had become a flood, and when on 24 January 2010 the *News of the World* said they had split and already agreed the details of the break-up, they decided enough was enough and began legal proceedings against the weekly newspaper. The couple's lawyer, Keith Schilling, slammed the 'widely republished' allegations as 'false and intrusive', adding that the paper had failed to meet 'reasonable demands' for an apology. He said the couple had also asked for a retraction of the allegations, which had subsequently been 'widely republished by mainstream news outlets'. The statement added that Sorrell Trope – who had been identified in the media as the divorce lawyer handling the split – had never actually met the couple. 'I have had no contact from . . . Angelina Jolie and/or Brad Pitt,' said Trope in a letter quoted in the statement. I have never met . . . your clients or had any involvement with either of them. The foregoing is true with respect to all other members of this firm.' Indeed, when the story of the split first hit the streets, Pitt and Jolie were apparently enjoying a meal together in Los Angeles. Jolie's father – now back in touch with his daughter, of course – also insisted that the stories were complete 'nonsense'.

Following their presence at the Directors Guild ceremony outlined in the prologue of this book, the couple put on another colourful show of unity when they took their eight-year-old son Maddox to the Super Bowl in Miami. There the couple, who were the talk of the Sun Life Stadium as they watched the New Orleans Saints take on the Indianapolis Colts, became the talk of the evening too, with their tactile behaviour sparking contrasting interpretations. 'Brad and Angelina looked perfectly happy together – so much so that it seems impossible that there were all of those recent reports they were separating,' said an eyewitness. 'On the other hand, they might have been overdoing it a little with the display of affection.'

The speculation about their relationship had clearly unsettled them, but Pitt was, as is so often the case, able to joke about it. As he left the Toy Crazy store in Malibu he put on a show for the watching paparazzi, reportedly grabbing his male friend's arm and joking, 'We're back together,' before pushing his friend away and saying, 'Now we're broken up.' With Valentine's Day just around the corner, Jolie was said to have purchased a 200-year-old olive tree for Pitt to plant at their French chateau. With the olive branch a widely recognized symbol of peace, it was felt that as well as being a romantic gesture, it might also be a conciliatory one.

Pitt and Jolie might not like the term Brangelina, but the power, fame, wealth and influence they have acquired under its umbrella is immense. Perhaps the greatest measure of their pre-eminence is that they have no obvious successors. The fact that comedian Russell Brand and singer Katy Perry have been mentioned as 'the next Brangelina' demonstrates just how far ahead of the galaxy of stars Pitt and Jolie are. Both of them must wonder how they came to be in such a pre-eminent position. For Pitt, who first pitched up in Hollywood after whimsically dropping his ambition to become a journalist, his journey to world-renowned supercouple seems far from inevitable. Had he not been involved in that minor car accident shortly before he changed career paths, might he now have been reporting on the lives of famous celebrities rather than actually being one? Jolie's place at the top of the celebrity tree seems far more predictable. True, both have suffered from, and at times despised, their fame, but Jolie is a more natural star than Pitt, who remains, to a large degree, a wholesome Midwestern boy. However much Jolie vows to scale down or abandon her movie career, she will surely never be happy unless she is in the spotlight. Perhaps, in the final analysis, her and Pitt do have a future together, but only as long as he's willing to stay in the public eye.

In February 2010 the family travelled to the Italian city of Venice, and as always their every move was stalked by the press. After all the rumours of discord, their time there was remarkable mostly for being unremarkable. They were spotted taking their children – who were carrying crayons and colouring-in books – to Jolie's favourite ice-cream parlour in the city, La Gelateria Lo Squero. Venice is, above all, a city of romance, but it also has a mysterious, tragic side to it. If the love story of Brad Pitt and Angelina Jolie has two dominant themes, they are romance and mystery.

One can only hope that tragedy does not become part of the gripping plot, as it has for so many people whose lives have enraptured the public. As the family tucked into their gelati, the world continued to be fascinated by their lives – and by what comes next for the most famous couple in the world . . .

Select Bibliography

Angelina Jolie: Portrait of a Superstar by Rhona Mercer
(John Blake Publishing, 2009)

Brad Pitt: the Rise to Stardom by Brian J Robb
(Plexus Publishing, 2002)

*Brangelina: The Untold Story of Brad Pitt and Angelina
Jolie* by Ian Halperin (Transit Publishing, 2009)

Jennifer: the Unauthorized Biography by Sean Smith
(Pan Macmillan, 2008)

Picture Credits

Inset 1

Inset 2